OTHER TITLES IN THE SERIES

DRY GLAZES

Jeremy Jernegan

A & C Black • London

University of Pennsylvania Press • Philadelphia

COVER (FRONT) *Untitled Buoy Group*, Jeremy Jernegan, 1995. 86 × 101.5 × 15cm (34 × 40 × 6in.). Glazed with various glazes including B5A with varied colourants, BL5A and BL14. Fired to cone 06. *Photo by the artist.*

COVER (BACK) *Teapot with Passive Spout (Suppressed Volume Series Black on White)*, Harris Deller, 2005. Black and white terra sigillata, fired to cone 10 (E21, p.48). 25 × 23 × 7.5cm (10 × 9 × 3in.). *Photo by the artist.*

FRONTISPIECE *Large Orange Bowl*, John Oles, 2008. Porcelain glazed with MC32 sprayed over MC31 (see p.92). Fired to cone 9. 30 × 25 cm (12 × 10 in.). *Photo by the artist.*

First published in Great Britain in 2009
A & C Black Publishers Limited
36 Soho Square
London W1D 3QY
www.acblack.com

ISBN 978-0-7136-7671-6

Published simultaneously in the USA by
University of Pennsylvania Press
3905 Spruce Street
Philadelphia, Pennsylvania 19104-4112

ISBN 978-0-8122-2097-1

Copyright © Jeremy Jernegan 2009

CIP Catalogue records for this book are available from the British Library and the US Library of Congress.

Typeset in 10 on 12pt Photina
Book design by Susan McIntyre
Cover design by Sutchinda Thompson

Printed and bound in China

This book is produced using paper that is made from wood grown in managed, sustainable forests. It is natural, renewable and recyclable. The logging and manufacturing processes conform to the environmental regulations of the country of origin.

Contents

Acknowledgements

I want to thank the many people who helped me with this project, especially the artists who so generously contributed images of their work and shared their formulas and techniques. There was a time in our field when glaze formulas and process information were closely guarded as trade secrets. I am proud that we have largely moved past that point, and as artists we understand that process is a part of what we do but is ultimately in service to ideas. The open exchange of information has benefited us all, and has certainly been a help for me in assembling this book. Finally, I want to acknowledge the important role my students have played in this project. Some of the formulas presented are the results of student assignments and experimentation over the last two decades. It has been my privilege to work with some very smart, gifted and inspiring students here at Tulane University, and I am grateful for their enthusiasm, curiosity and input. Special thanks go to Kate Keelen for her assistance in glaze-mixing and copy input, and my wife Vicki for proof-reading and unwavering encouragement. I also want to thank Tulane's Committee on Research for its support of this project.

Untitled Form, Jeremy Jernegan, 1983. 8 × 20cm (3 × 8in.). Glazed with CO22 and raku-fired to cone 05 with moderate post-firing reduction. *Photo by the author.*

Introduction

Glaze is glass, as I repeatedly tell my students. A proper glaze is compounded from silica, alumina and one or more fluxing oxides. Proper glazes are uniformly smooth and glossy, and fit the clay body correctly. These ideal coatings are insoluble, durable and hard. Such glazes are valuable for any ceramicist making tableware, sanitary ware or many other utilitarian applications. This book is not primarily concerned with such optimal or ideal glazes, but rather with what the potter Jim Robinson once humorously referred to as 'ludicrous glazes': those compelling, fired surfaces that are objectively under-fired, oversaturated with a particular oxide, or represent such an extreme composition balance as to be nearly absurd when set against the usual canon of glaze formulation.

Many dry glazes lie at the extreme borders of glaze formulation. Some are not really glazes at all, but fused crusts of alumina and flux, or colouring oxides combined with flux in very high proportions of each. These surfaces may be less durable than conventional glazes and are usually unsuitable for use with food, but they are often texturally varied and visually rich. This book focuses on both the very dry end of the glaze spectrum – those sintered clays, engobes and glazes with barely a hint of glassy character – and the more familiar devitrified matt glazes produced with the

Deep Breath, Bradley Sabin, 2002. Glazed with SE41 (p.118) on cagework. Flowers glazed with commercial underglazes and BL18 (p.74). Fired to cone 04. 81 × 81 × 30cm (32 × 32 × 12in.). *Photo by the artist.*

oxides of calcium, magnesium, barium and strontium. There is a great deal of interesting work that can be done with the clay surface alone, with no added coatings. Burnished, smoked, reduced or sandblasted, the raw clay is also a dry surface, but it is not one I am addressing here, except as it pertains to application techniques and colour response. This book is concerned with the applied and fired ceramic surface that fuses enough to remain stable and permanent, but is not glossy in a conventional way.

The need for dry glazes is perhaps greatest in sculptural applications. As more ceramic artists explore ideas less related to pottery, the interest in non-glassy surfaces increases.

Though countless thousands of exquisite pots have been finished without a glassy surface, particularly in ancient times, nevertheless it is glass coatings

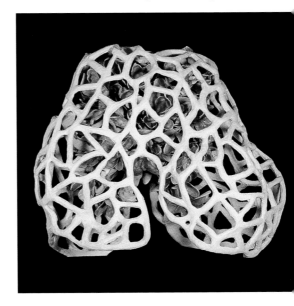

Song of a Drunken Angel (detail),
Arthur Gonzales, 2007. Commercial glazes
and slips mixed variously with kaolin, borax
and frits. Single-fired to cone 1 reduction.
178 × 107 × 43cm (70 × 42 × 17in.).
Photo by John Wilson White.

that are nearly synonymous with pots
and other utilitarian applications of clay.
As a contemporary ceramic artist, I see
the selection of a surface as significant in
more than one way. Aside from the
formal qualities of tonal value, colour
and texture, the coating on a contemporary sculpture signals a range of
potential associations and meanings.
Certainly, surface can have important
specific associative qualities – useful in
alluding to another material such as
metal or stone. More broadly, however,
the glossy glaze surface tends to bring
pots and traditions of potters readily to
mind, while the dry surface does not.
This observation carries no implication of
hierarchy in terms of pots and sculpture,

but simply acknowledges the familiar
associations of certain kinds of objects.

My premise in organizing this book is to
examine the potentials for non-glossy,
fired ceramic surfaces, without particular
concern for conventional notions of
correct formulations or appropriate
hardness, fusion, maturation, etc. The
criteria for determining the desirability of a
given glaze surface are left to the artist. To
paraphrase the familiar quote from Duke
Ellington, 'If it looks good, it is good.'

This book is intended to provide a framework for understanding the types of dry-
glaze surfaces possible, illustrated with
glaze formulas (also known as recipes),
tests and examples. There are many fine
reference volumes that treat glaze calculation in considerable detail, as well as
providing greater specificity about the
range of major and minor glaze materials
we use in compounding glazes. I present
the major materials associated with matt
and dry glaze effects, but I am not seeking
to provide a comprehensive overview of
the field. For this and other approaches, I
direct readers to the reference section and
some of the many great volumes available.

About the glaze formula notations

Glazes listed here are identified by a code
number that is keyed to the illustration,
their name and Orton firing cone, and
attributed, in parentheses, to the individual who developed or significantly
modified the glaze (if known) or provided
me with it. The firing atmosphere is
neutral unless specified as reduction (R)
or post-firing reduction (PFR). There are
a number of glazes in general use with no
clear attribution, as there are many similar variants of other popular formulas. I
am grateful to all the artists who have
shared their formulas with me for

publication in this book. I have made every effort to correctly attribute glazes to their inventors, and if there are any omissions they are both unintended and regretted. Formulas for each glaze are shown on the opposite page in the same position.

A standard notation for ceramic formulas is to express the formula with all ingredients for the glaze base totaling 100%, and any colourants or modifiers added as percentages following the total. This format is said to be in base unity, and makes it easy to see the proportional breakdown of the glaze as percentages of the total. It also makes it easier to experiment with colour by substituting different colouring oxides or stains without changing the base. I have followed the same standard in the formulas in this book, with some exceptions. One problem with this approach is its assumption of a clear glass base that works without the colourants as well as with them. Most of the glazes in this book have no clear glass base, and a number of them are configured to have such an excess of colourant that the final glaze-surface result is dependent on the colourant. A few of the glazes are primarily colouring oxide, in which case there is no glaze without the 'colourants'. For those reasons some glazes are expressed as a single formula totaling 100, while most are a unity base formula followed by the colouring oxides and suspension agents.

Illustrations of artists' work are included to provide examples of the applications of glazes to various surfaces, and to connect the lab work with actual uses by artists. In most cases formulas for the surface on the work illustrated are provided, usually in the same chapter. The glaze reference and page number(s) and application information are noted in the caption and refer to a glaze formula listed at the end of the chapter, for example

Standing Mark, Jeremy Jernegan, 1994. Ceramic and steel. Glazed with copper-oxide wash applied and wiped off with E16 (see p.52) on top. Fired to cone 04. 221 × 43 × 40.5cm (87 × 17 × 16in.). *Photo by the artist.*

'glazed with SE41, (p.118)' found in Chapter 9 special effects (SE) glaze set. Illustrations of glaze tests conducted by the author are also included, to provide an immediate visual communication of the information covered, as well as a quick reference for artists seeking surface solutions for their work. The tiles were made from a stoneware clay body and were dipped halfway in a porcelain slip to provide information about results on white and iron-based clay bodies. In some cases the glaze is so opaque there is no apparent difference in the surfaces of slipped and non-slipped tiles. Glazes were applied by pouring a single uniform coat over the tile to minimise variation from brush-strokes. Glaze photographs were taken by the author.

High calcium matt with rutile and iron showing clusters of small titanium crystals, MC28A1 (p.92), Orton cone 10R. *Photo by the author.*

Chapter 1

What makes a dry glaze dry?

Quite a few things can make a glaze matt or dry, although there are four general glaze phenomena that result in a variety of surfaces, from fluid but opaque to extremely dry. Before discussing the different physical structures of dry glazes, it is helpful to have a clear understanding of the 'ideal' glossy glaze, and how it is formed. For example, the popular Binn's Clear is a well-balanced glaze that fires transparent at cone 10. During the firing, a stoneware glaze like this one goes through a series of stages as the temperature rises. The finely ground particles of silica flour, potash feldspar, whiting, kaolin and zinc first sinter, or begin to fuse, forming a 'cohesive mass without (yet) melting'.[1]

The sintering process occurs in firing all clays and glaze materials, and is affected by the particle size as well as the presence of fluxes. The melting process begins as the heat breaks down the bonds within the molecules of each particle of the glaze, and the fluxing oxides begin to interact with the compounds of alumina and silica. The interaction of materials can be quite complex as they melt, forming eutectics that promote more rapid melting; a eutectic describes a phenomenon in which the interaction of two (or more) materials results in a melting point lower than that of either constituent material.

Gases liberated from the chemical decomposition of materials form bubbles and serve to stir the mixture, as does the movement created through convection of the increasingly liquid glaze.[2] This process continues until all the material is completely dissolved into a liquid glass matrix. The finer the materials are ground, the more rapidly and completely this occurs. The gases liberated through chemical decomposition and interactions between the materials, as well as air trapped between particles and the clay body layer during the glaze application, result in small and large bubbles in the glass. Some glazes liberate so much gas that they appear to go through a boiling phase during the melt, with bubbles forming and bursting on the glaze surface. Normally, the glaze has time to off-gas all the bubbles and attains a fully melted and transparent state at the maximum firing temperature before the kiln is shut off and begins to cool. The liquid glass is transparent and glossy at this point.

The initial crystalline molecular structure of the materials that make up the glaze – silica, alumina, potassium, calcium, zinc, etc. – has been broken by the heat of firing, and the resulting liquid mass of molecular compounds has assumed an amorphous or random state. Liquids differ from solids in that they have no crystalline structure and so appear clear. Most materials that melt when heated re-crystallise when they cool, and appear opaque. Silica, the basis of most glazes, has a particular tendency to remain in an amorphous state upon cooling, particularly if the cooling cycle is quite fast. In addition,

Covered Jar Column Series, Val Cushing, 2001. Lid and base glazed with 50:50 mix of MC40 and MC39 (p.88), the rest with MC42, fired to cone 10. 91cm (36in.) tall. *Photo by Seth Tice Lewis.*

and has the glossy surface typical of a fluid material.[4]

Matt and dry glazes result when the glass-forming process is altered by any of a number of variables, from the glaze composition to the firing temperature and cooling cycle. To examine the primary types of dry glazes, I will begin with those most similar to an ideal clear glass, and move to those at the extreme end of the spectrum.

Crystalline matts: devitrified glazes

During the process of cooling, some compounds may dissociate themselves from the general melted glass and redevelop a crystalline structure. This is known generally as devitrification, the extent of which can vary from subtle to very pronounced. Some metallic oxides have a greater tendency than others to devitrify into a crystalline state. When added in sufficient quantity, the fluxing oxides of calcium, magnesium, barium, strontium and zinc will facilitate the growth of very tiny crystals in the glaze matrix, resulting in an opaque glaze with a surface texture ranging from a smooth eggshell to that of a dry, river-tumbled stone. The surface texture results from the particular size and type of crystalline structure generated by the fluxing oxides in the formula, and their relative quantities. Each oxide also has a particular influence on colour development in the glaze, from the muted and pastel hues in a magnesium-rich glaze to the vivid and intense colours of barium-rich glazes. This type of matt glaze can show evidence of fluidity, even to the extent of running down on vertical surfaces, because it was completely melted prior to the growth of the crystals that give it the matt appearance.

liquids of high viscosity, such as melted glazes, tend to cool sufficiently rapidly that recrystallisation does not occur.[3] So in a typical clear glaze, the liquid glass chills upon cooling and freezes in its amorphous form, resulting in a super-cooled liquid which is transparent

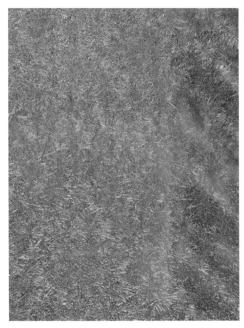

Remarkably large titanium crystals growing in an iron-saturate calcium matt containing 40% titanium dioxide. Cone 10R (MC30C, p.92).

A dense matt of zinc crystals form a crust on this high-zinc glaze at cone 6 (glaze MC19E, p.16). *Photos by the author.*

Other metal oxides used primarily as colouring or opacifying oxides can also promote the growth of crystal structures in and on the surface of cooling glazes. Titanium, for instance, introduced into a glaze as titanium dioxide or rutile will frequently grow as small but visible crystals floating on the surface of a liquid glass beneath. When the glaze cools the crystalline surface may appear quite flat and dry, at times almost textured due to the layer of interlocking crystals. In some cases the crystals do not cover the entire surface, but create patches and highlights dotted with crystals. These glazes are often called 'microcrystalline', a reference to the visible character of the crystal growth. Slow cooling tends to promote the growth of crystals in all glazes, but particularly so with larger crystals.

It is not uncommon to see glaze-firing results from a slow-cooling hard-brick kiln appear quite different from those of a rapidly cooling fibre kiln. Macrocrystalline glazes are a special variant of glazes with visible crystals in which the glaze formula is particularly low in alumina oxide and the glaze is held in a fluid state, usually with an electronic controller, for an extended period to promote the formation of very large crystals. The illustration on p.17 (right column) shows a reasonably fluid cone 6 glaze fluxed with sodium frit, calcium and zinc oxide, to which increasing amounts of zinc oxide are added. The zinc encourages the growth of isolated zinc crystals, then a solid mass of needle crystals floating on the surface, and finally the excess zinc inhibits the ability of the glaze to melt completely, yielding an opaque glaze with undissolved material.

Partially melted glazes: under-fired or high-alumina/high-silica glazes

If a glaze formula is excessively high in alumina or silica (relative to its firing temperature), it may not be able to melt completely. The process of fusion is well progressed, but the chemical balance of the glaze is such that not all the material can dissolve into a fully melted glass; the partially dissolved components maintain their original crystalline structure and give the glaze an opaque look. Depending on the degree of the imbalance the resulting surface may be completely fused but matt white, or quite opaque, dry and somewhat textured.

Aluminum oxide is an important component in glazes, adding a stiffness to the melt that is necessary to keep a glass from flowing off the vertical surface of a pot or sculpture. The presence of alumina is often cited as the primary difference between ceramic glazes and glass used in art and industry, which has virtually no alumina oxide. Normally, the quantity of alumina in a transparent glaze is fairly small. A molecular ratio of 1:10, alumina to silica, is common for stoneware glazes, and considerably less is used in earthenware. Alumina oxide has a very high melting point, 2050°C (3722°F), and requires the combination of more active melting oxides to melt it into the silica glass matrix. As the quantity of alumina in a formula is increased, the balance between alumina, silica and flux shifts, and the resulting glaze becomes increasingly stiff, opaque and dry, until it may not appear to melt at all at the given temperature. As Herman Seger observed, 'Little alumina gives high mobility: too much alumina will yield a melt that is too viscous and will be matt, dull and immature when cooled.'[5] Glazes that are very high in alumina look more like engobes or slips than glaze, and in some ways they are. Kaolin, the pure clay that is often the primary source of alumina in glazes, is composed of alumina and silica in a 1:2 molecular proportion – Al_2O_3 $2SiO_2$.

Silica also has a high melting point, 1600°C (2917°F), and while it is the primary glass former in a glaze, it requires the addition of sufficient fluxing oxides to get it to melt at the kinds of temperatures normally chosen by ceramic artists. If silica is introduced to a glaze in excess quantities (relative to the fluxing oxides) the glaze may not fully melt, resulting in a surface that can range from frosty opaque to stony. Silica may be introduced to glazes as a 325 mesh, 200 mesh (as is the case with all the formulas in this book) – or 100 mesh powder. The mesh size refers to the number of holes per square inch in a screen it can pass through. If larger-grain silica flour is used, such as 100 mesh, it tends to slow the melting process, which may result in a partially melted matt glaze.

The amount of alumina and silica in a 'normal' glaze is directly related to its intended firing temperature. The hotter the firing, the less fluxing oxide is required and the more alumina is added to control fluidity. If a given glaze is under-fired, that ratio of alumina and silica is no longer considered appropriate for the amount of fluxing oxides, and the glaze may appear opaque and dry. For that reason, a fluid glaze fired at its normal temperature may be seen as a high-alumina/high-silica matt when intentionally under-fired.

Under various conditions, excess quantities of other glaze ingredients including feldspar, bone ash or talc may also fail to dissolve completely in a glaze, which will also lead to a matt and opaque surface. C.W. Parmalee refers to a related

Examples of four types of dry glazes: (top left) MC34 (p.84), a sintered matt; (top right) MC22A2 (p.90), a crystalline matt; (bottom left) MC22 (p.84), a partially melted matt; and (bottom right) A13B (p.62), a flux-saturated matt.

interruption that may occur during the melting process, which he refers to as a 'false immiscibility', where the more fluid and fusible portion of the glaze separates from the rest and is then absorbed into the porous clay body 'or it forms a glassy magma surrounding the partially fused or undissolved portions of the glaze'.[6] This is partly caused by uneven blending of raw materials, and the body absorption may be more likely with a porous and refractory bisque-fired stoneware, such as might be used for raku-firing.

In his book *Revealing Glazes*, Ian Currie explains his excellent approach to testing and understanding glazes based on what he calls a standard recipe grid system. Currie uses a rectangular grid framework to organise a series of step tests that illustrate the behaviour of the major constituents of any glaze as they mix in different proportions. While the basic system of step tests structured into triaxials and quadraxials is common and widely used, Currie has simplified it and, most importantly, established useful ratios of materials for the four-corner starting points. I have found his system very helpful in identifying dry-glaze potential and seeing the ratios of alumina, silica and flux that result in these surfaces.

The illustration on p. 17 shows glaze

ILLUSTRATION PAGE 17
Left column from top to bottom, B30A–B30E, increasing silica in barium matt;
Centre column, B31A–B31E, increasing alumina in a barium matt;
Right column, MC19B–MC19F, increasing zinc in a sodium/calcium/zinc matt.
All fired to cone 6.

B30A – cone 6		B31A – cone 6		MC19B – cone 6	
Barium carb.	37.3	Barium carb.	28.2	Frit 3110	20
G200 spar	56	G200 spar	42.2	Zinc oxide	20
EPKaolin	6.7	EPKaolin	5.4	Whiting	20
Silica	0	Silica	24.2	Silica	36
	100		100	Bentonite	4
					100
Copper carb.	3	Copper carb.	3	Copper carb.	2

B30B – cone 6		B31B – cone 6		MC19C – cone 6	
Barium carb.	32.7	Barium carb.	26.3	Frit 3110	19
G200 spar	49.2	G200 spar	39.6	Zinc oxide	23.8
EPKaolin	6	EPKaolin	10.8	Whiting	19
Silica	12.1	Silica	23.3	Silica	34.3
	100		100	Bentonite	3.8
					100
Copper carb.	3	Copper carb.	3	Copper carb.	2

B30C – cone 6		B31C – cone 6		MC19C – cone 6	
Barium carb.	28.2	Barium carb.	24.5	Frit 3110	19
G200 spar	42.2	G200 spar	36.8	Zinc oxide	23.8
EPKaolin	5.4	EPKaolin	16.2	Whiting	19
Silica	24.2	Silica	22.5	Silica	34.3
	100		100	Bentonite	3.8
					100
Copper carb.	3	Copper carb.	3	Copper carb.	2

B30D – cone 6		B31D – cone 6		MC19E – cone 6	
Barium carb.	23.6	Barium carb.	22.6	Frit 3110	17.4
G200 spar	35.4	G200 spar	34	Zinc oxide	30.4
EPKaolin	4.8	EPKaolin	21.7	Whiting	17.4
Silica	36.2	Silica	21.7	Silica	31.3
	100		100	Bentonite	3.4
					100
Copper carb.	3	Copper carb.	3	Copper carb.	2

B30E – cone 6		B31E – cone 6		MC19F – cone 6	
Barium carb.	19	Barium carb.	20.8	Frit 3110	16
G200 spar	28.5	G200 spar	31.3	Zinc oxide	36
EPKaolin	4.2	EPKaolin	27.1	Whiting	16
Silica	48.3	Silica	20.8	Silica	28.8
	100		100	Bentonite	3.2
					100
Copper carb.	3	Copper carb.	3	Copper carb.	2

Thrown Square Box, Patrick Horsley. Glazed with MC19. 10 × 18 × 18cm (4 × 7 × 7in.). Photo by Dan Kivitka.

tiles that were part of a standard grid that blended barium carbonate, potash feldspar, kaolin and silica, all coloured with 3% copper and fired to cone 6. I have selected them because they shed particular light on the role of silica and alumina, and how their ratios can shift a glaze from a sintered matt to a gloss, to a partially melted matt. That specific progression can be seen in the left-hand column, tiles B30A–E. As the formulas show, B30A is rich in flux (37% barium and 56% feldspar) but has no additional silica, and the result is a dry sintered matt. Tiles B30B–D add silica, with modest decreases in barium and spar, and the result is a glossy, nearly fluid glaze. With the bottom tile, B30E, the quantity of added silica is up to 48%, and the result is a stiff, partially melted matt that illustrates how refractory silica can be when added in excess. The quantity of alumina is modest and nearly constant throughout these tests.

In the centre-column series of tiles, B31A–E, the quantity of silica is nearly constant, and the amount of alumina increases in five steps from top to bottom. Test 31A is the same relatively balanced glaze as 30C with 5.4% kaolin, but as the amount of kaolin (supplying alumina) increases, the glaze becomes a partially melted matt, then finally, with 32% kaolin in 31E, a very dry sintered matt. It is also interesting to see how increasing alumina modifies the colour response of the copper in the glaze from a green-blue to a muted brown.

Sintered matts: significantly under-fired glazes

Sintered matts may be seen as the lowest-temperature end of the spectrum of high-alumina/high-silica matts. The physical distinction between them is that no real melt has occurred. These glazes are fired only hot enough to sinter or stick the ingredients together into a hard coating, but not to melt them, resulting in a class of matt glazes that have a very dry surface, looking more like fired clay than glass. It is these surfaces that the Oregon potter Jim Robinson once humorously referred to as 'ludicrous glazes', because they are so far from the normal standards of a proper glaze. During the firing, the sintering process causes the materials to interact sufficiently to become a relatively hard surface that adheres to the clay body beneath and will still develop a range of colours from ceramic colouring oxides. Because the degree of fusion is so slight, colour development tends to be limited and favours pastel shades. Sintered matts may have any of a number of fluxing oxide compositions, each of which will influence colour in a different way. In some cases a formula may contain fluxes with a granular character, such as borax or lithium carbonate, which will melt at a lower temperature, causing a spotting or speckling of melted areas within the glaze surface.

Application over metal oxides like copper or other glazes may encourage the sintered matts toward greater fusion and darker, more saturated surfaces. Sintered matt surfaces are relatively soft, particularly those formed at earthenware temperatures, and can be abraded or chipped off. In most cases they are unsatisfactory for utilitarian use and should be reserved for purely aesthetic applications.

Flux-saturated, low-silica matts and oxide crusts

Silica is generally considered essential to forming a glass, although lead and boron, two oxides primarily used as fluxes, will melt into a transparent pseudo-glaze without it. If a glaze is formulated with high amounts of fluxing oxides like lithium, sodium or potassium, or colouring oxides like copper, cobalt, iron or manganese, and little to no silica, it may fuse into an opaque crust with little glasslike character. In relation to the ideal glaze, this mixture is badly starved of silica, and while a melting process does occur the result is not a glass but rather a crust of melted oxides. Additionally, in some cases the melting point of the glaze flux is relatively high by itself, and requires eutectic interaction with silica to lower it to a point where a complete melt may occur. With inadequate quantities of silica the melt is incomplete. These flux-saturated glazes represent extremes of glaze formulation, with the normal ratios of silica/alumina and flux turned upside down. Fluxing oxides profoundly affect colour development, and high concentrations can result in dramatic and surprising effects. Fired surfaces can range from what appears to be a coloured staining of the clay with little depth, to a crusty and opaque or metallic surface.

These four categories are a way to understand the primary physical differences between the various dry surfaces available, and all make specific reference to the model glossy glaze as a point of departure. Inevitably, the need to generalise in order to create understandable groupings has led me to simplify the complex reality of the glaze chemistry involved. It is also true that some glazes can be described as fitting more than one category. In fact, several of the examples given in this book might be described as flux-saturated and sintered-matt glazes or partially melted and crystalline matts. However, I hope the categories are helpful and provide a way to understand the phenomena that result in the wide spectrum of dry glazes that we use.

The final appearance of a dry glaze is determined to a large degree by its dominant fluxing and colouring oxides, as well as the temperature and atmosphere in which it is fired. Thus this book is organised primarily into chapters defined by the dominant fluxing oxides. In each chapter there may be several or all of the major types of dry glazes. Grouping by dominant fluxing oxide is also something of a simplification, because in many cases glazes have three or more fluxes contributing to the melt and the final characteristics of the glaze. Nevertheless, I find this type of organisation useful in recognising general characteristics of the glazes. Within each chapter, illustrated glaze tests are grouped by firing temperature, typically cone 10 reduction, cone 6 and cone 06–04.

Life Support, Jeremy Jernegan, 1988. Monoprinted drawing with black chalk (E13), E29 with various stain colours used on the structure. Fired to cone 04. 71 × 36 × 31cm (28 × 14 × 12in.). *Photo by the artist.*

Chapter 2
Health and safety

A number of the most interesting glazes in this book were developed by testing seemingly extreme formulas to see what resulted. This sort of empirical investigation is a great way to learn about glazes and discover new surfaces, but it can also expose the ceramic artist to a number of health hazards. It is important to be aware of the dangers that you face when working with ceramic materials and to do what you can to protect yourself. Some materials, such as lead, are particularly poisonous, and while the risks of handling such a material can be minimised they may not be entirely eliminated. It is ultimately up to the informed individual to determine what risks he/she is willing to take in pursuing their art. You can elect to limit the materials in the glaze palette to those with moderate to low toxicity, and still have a rich array of glazes to work with. The scope of glazes presented in this book is fairly comprehensive, and assumes the reader will take appropriate steps to protect themselves when handling, mixing, applying and firing the glazes listed here. Additionally, there can be real hazards in using inappropriate glazes for surfaces that will come into contact with food or drink. Many dry glazes do not resist acid attack well, with the result that toxic metallic oxides may find their way into food. While some of the glazes in this book are balanced, stable and food-safe, the formulas are presented primarily for sculptural applications and should be considered unfit for food contact unless specifically approved.

With the exception of chapters 1, 2 and 3, each chapter in the book introduces one or more fluxing oxides and a selection of glazes making use of them. The relative toxicity and particular hazards of working with each one are outlined. There is also considerable information available on glaze toxicity, and interested readers are encouraged to investigate the subject further via the reference section of this volume.

Industrial hygienists refer to most of the glaze hazards we encounter in the lab as either *chronic* exposure hazards or hazards of *acute* toxicity. The former term describes dangers arising from long-term exposure to what may seem a low-grade hazard: for example, breathing clay or silica dust over time (usually many years) can and does result in lung damage known as silicosis. The latter term refers to materials such as lead, barium, cadmium and chromium that are highly poisonous: ingestion of significant amounts can cause immediate illness.

Both types of hazard deserve our respect and attention, though in glaze mixing and use we must be particularly cautious about acute toxicity hazards. Materials and glazes that have such toxicity are identified in this book with the indication (toxic) after their name. Material Safety Data Sheets (MSDS) are available for all clay and glaze materials. Your distributor can provide them, and

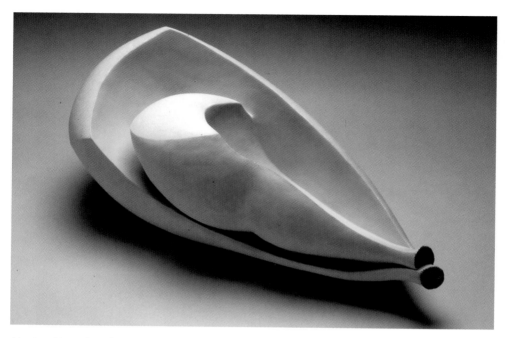

Nesting Green Succulent, Lisa Conway, 2005. A20 (p.62) on exterior, fired to cone 04. 46 × 86 × 46cm (18 × 34 × 18in.). *Photo by Grace Weston.*

many can be downloaded from a manufacturer's website. The MSDS lists all the hazards associated with each material. Employers must maintain a complete and current file of the MSDS for each material a worker may encounter in the workplace.

The first line of defence in protecting yourself from hazards in the studio is to use appropriate personal protective equipment and observe good hygienic work practices. For the ceramic artist this means wearing a well-fitting dust mask or respirator that at least meets the N-95 OSHA standard (this is the designation of a type of dust mask that meets the basic standard for 'nuisance dusts' by the Occupational and Safety Health Administration, the US federal agency overseeing worker health and safety; it is noted on the packaging of dust masks in the US), a full-length apron, closed shoes, long sleeves and rubber gloves. The studio work area should be separated from any living area, and kept clean through frequent wiping with a wet sponge or mopping to eliminate dusts. Glaze materials should be kept in clearly labelled closed containers, and any spills should be wiped up immediately.

It is important to be aware of the potential for exposure to the materials we use. The three primary routes of exposure are inhalation, ingestion and absorption.

Inhalation is perhaps the most obvious threat, because we are working with powdered materials when we mix glazes. These powders are often very fine and, when disturbed by opening a bag, weighing, screening, etc., their dusts may remain airborne for quite a while.

Untitled, Sally Brogden, 1992. Glazed with similar glaze to SE5A (p.120). 40 × 20 × 20cm (16 × 8 × 8in.). *Photo by the artist.*

To minimise the danger of breathing dusts, a dust mask or respirator should be worn and glaze-mixing work should be done in a booth with an effective exhaust system that immediately removes the dust before it can circulate in the room. Chemical fume hoods are excellent for this purpose, though they are also expensive and may not always be available. A localised exhaust hood can be useful, too, provided it is kept close to the work area. As soon as glazes are weighed out, they should be mixed with water to a wet-to-creamy consistency before screening or further mixing. Once the glaze is wet the dust-inhalation hazard is eliminated. Applying glazes with a spray gun should only be done in a powerful spray booth that will exhaust all the dusts from the work area. Glazes high in lead should not be sprayed due to the toxicity of the dusts.

During the firing process toxic fumes containing carbon monoxide, sulphur, fluorine, lead, etc. may be liberated from the kiln into the surrounding space. Kiln rooms must be well ventilated to the outside and separated from the regular work area. Additional hazards can occur with the use of high-lead glazes when the fuming of the glaze deposits a thin layer of lead oxide onto the walls of the kiln, which may later be disturbed and inhaled by the ceramic artist.

Ingestion of materials occurs when airborne dusts are swallowed, or dust and glaze are transferred from the artist's hands to food, drink or cigarettes, and then to the mouth. You should never eat, drink or smoke when mixing or using glazes. Ingestion can also occur with food or drink contacting fired-glaze surfaces that are not properly formulated and fired to be food-safe. Unless you are sure a glaze is food-safe, it should not be used where it may come into contact with food or drink.

Wearing an apron when mixing and using glazes will protect you from soiling street clothes and transporting toxic materials into the home where they may contaminate the living environment. Closed shoes should be wiped off or left at the studio to avoid tracking spilled materials outside. Clothing that is soiled with glaze should be washed separately from other laundry to avoid cross-contaminating other clothing.

Absorption of toxic material can occur when glaze materials penetrate the skin through cuts or damaged areas. Limiting skin exposure is the best protection. Use rubber gloves when handling materials and glaze, avoid stirring glazes with your hands, and wear long sleeves and long trousers. The alkaline glaze fluxes, for example, are not particularly toxic, but their high pH can cause severe drying and irritation of the skin. Washing your hands well when completing work, and showering to remove dusts from the hair, etc., will help remove any glaze residue and ensure the glaze compounds pose no further risk.

Environmental concerns

Discarding excess glaze and glaze tests without contaminating landfills and groundwater with potentially hazardous material is a significant problem for larger users such as schools and community studios. One effective way to neutralise the hazard is to collect all glaze waste in a bucket; when this is full, pour off the water and let the residue dry. Next throw and bisque-fire a sturdy stoneware crucible (or more than one if necessary) with a capacity of between a couple of quarts and a gallon. Then place the glaze waste into the fired crucible and slowly glaze-fire it up to about cone 5 (place a layer of waste brick under the crucible in case there is breakage or leaking). The waste glaze typically fuses into a mottled glass, rendering it inert, compact and safe to dispose of in a landfill.

RIGHT *Wisdom Over Folly*, Mikey Walsh, 2006. Glazed with A17 (p.62) over thick white slip, fired to cone 04. 76 x 25.5 x 10cm (30 x 10 x 4in.). *Photo by Kevin Duffy.*

Klaxon, Jeremy Jernegan, 2008. Earthenware and stainless steel. Tiles are monoprinted with black engobe and, after firing to cone 1, a variant of E16 (p.52) is applied, sanded when dry and fired to cone 04. 99 × 117 × 15cm (39 × 46 × 6in.). *Photo by Mike Smith.*

Chapter 3

Developing the surface and visual texture

Glossy glazes can develop remarkable visual depth through complex events of the melt producing varied opacity and the mottled distribution of colouring oxides in the glass layer. Additionally, the interaction between the clay body and the liquid glaze flowing over it can be pronounced and create patterns, runs, pooling glaze, etc. As nice as these effects can be, they are often difficult to orchestrate, such that the best areas of a piece may not be where you would choose to put them.

Typically, dry glazes are opaque and lose some of the illusion of depth common with fluid glazes. This necessarily changes your expectations and approach when working with them, but that loss is more than made up for by the ability to control and predict the outcome to a greater degree.

One of the important opportunities that dry glazes provide is the ability to work in layers and fire pieces multiple times, developing or modifying the surface until it works best with the form. Re-glazing and re-firing can be done with any glaze, but the application of water-based glaze is difficult on the glassy surface of conventional glaze, as it has no porosity and no 'tooth' to hold a fresh

layer without it running off. Another problem with conventional re-glazing is that a fluid glaze tends to move each time it is fired, particularly on vertical surfaces. One runs a risk of the base glaze shifting substantially in the re-firing, thereby changing its appearance. Finally, when a second or third layer is applied to a glossy glaze, the top layer tends to melt into the one below and be substantially diluted, in some cases seeming to disappear. Dry glaze surfaces are usually

Dry Blue Vase, Lana Wilson, 2007. Glazed with E12 (p.50), applied and wiped off. Fired to cone 6. *Photo by the artist.*

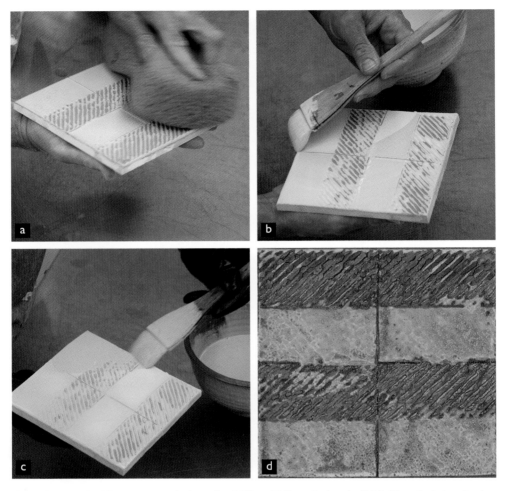

A tile is coated with copper wash (see tile CO2, p.130) and wiped off (a). The tile is brushed with a coat of yellow engobe (b), which is partially wiped away before the final coat of glaze A3 (p.64) is brushed on (c) and the tile is fired to cone 04 (d). The copper turns the glaze metallic, and the variation in thickness that comes from applying it with a brush creates significant variation in the fired glaze colour. *Photos by the author.*

stable and change less, making them more predictable and better suited to reapplication and re-firing.

Dry glazes are applied in all the usual ways: by dipping, pouring, brushing or spraying. However, the nature of the pieces and sometimes the glaze itself influences the choice of which technique to use. Dipping a piece usually provides the most uniform coverage, but it also requires a large quantity of glaze to cover most pieces. Some glazes do not remain in suspension well and must be stirred constantly, making them problematic for dipping. Pouring a glaze can be effective, though in covering an entire piece a poured glaze may create unintended multiple coats and drip marks. The test tiles in this book were all poured to achieve a uniform coat, which is easy to do and effective at that small scale.

Brushing on a glaze can be the most versatile and direct method of application, though it does require skill and patience to achieve a uniform coat. In general it is best to use a large soft Hake-style brush of natural fibre, which holds a good amount of glaze and allows you to flow it uniformly over a piece. Uneven, though potentially interesting glaze effects may also be developed by using an inexpensive stiff bristle brush for application. For example, Virginia Scotchie develops her rich crusty surfaces in part through mixing the glaze to a very thick consistency and applying it to the bisque ware by dabbing it on with a brush full of glaze (see p.123, chapter 10). I find the ability to reapply more

glaze in thin spots and re-fire work makes brush application more useful with dry than with conventional glazes.

Spraying glaze can be an effective method, but requires a compressor and a spray gun, as well as a spray booth to exhaust the glaze dust. Glazes need to be fairly liquid and well screened for spraying, and those with a coarse particle size, due to granular elements such as borax, cannot be sprayed. Spraying glazes allows a very even coating to be applied, even to vitrified surfaces, but it also requires skill and patience to build up an adequate coat and may be difficult on irregular shapes. Jim Robinson uses a spray gun to good effect, applying both uniform coats and thin, layered coatings of glaze, allowing him to vary both the density of glaze and the range of tones across the pieces (see image, p.98).

Tipping Points, Aurore Chabot, 2005. Blue sigillata on tips, Amaco Velvet underglazes and copper-oxide wash, fired to cone 04. 30 × 34 × 18cm (12 × 13½ × 7in.). *Photo by the artist.*

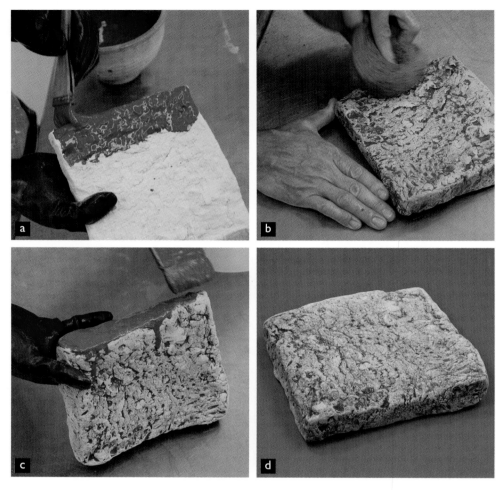

A bisque-fired piece is coated with a commercial blue underglaze, which is then wiped off (a & b). The piece is then brush-coated with a glaze rich in soda ash (A12, p.62) and fired to cone 06 (c & d). *Photos by the author.*

By layering one or more oxides and/or glazes on a piece of sculpture, an artist is able to physically exploit surface texture on a piece, highlighting areas through selective application and removal. The process of interacting physically with a piece while glazing has been important for me in activating a surface. Rather than expecting a glaze to create the final effect, I try to build up a surface that relates specifically to the form by layering it on and wiping it off.

When a glaze or slip coating is applied, it initially cloaks the form, potentially obscuring or camouflaging the piece. When removing an underglaze or oxide wash with a sponge or scrub pad, the abrasion allows the actual highlights of the form to be differentiated from the recesses. In most cases the underglaze hangs in the recesses, exaggerating and emphasising them. If the result is too subtle, it can be repeated. If it is too strong

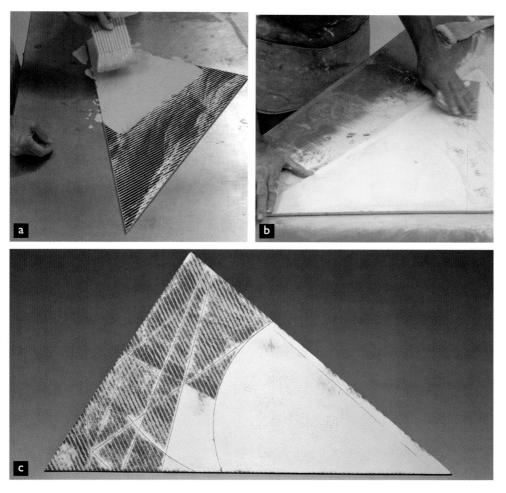

This tile was made using a silkscreen and monoprinting process with black engobe and earthenware casting slip that resulted in the graphic image and raised straight and arching lines on the surface of the tile. The fired tile was coated with white slip (E1, p.48) and allowed to dry (a). The slip was sanded away with medium-grit sandpaper (b) and re-fired to cone 04 (c). The subtle topography of the lines can be better emphasised by dry-sanding rather than sponging the surface.

it may be muted by applying an opaque glaze or engobe on top. The nature of the process is such that it allows revision and experimentation. This keeps glazing from becoming divorced from the hands-on involvement of making the forms, and allows you to articulate the nuances of form that may have been so central to the original fabrication. Selective removal can also reveal very subtle topographical changes in a surface and allow them to be amplified through value or colour contrasts. In some recent wall pieces I have applied layers of white slip to the surface of a vitrified screenprinted tile, and sanded back the surface to develop a graphic defined by raised lines in the tile surface (see above). Using sandpaper rather than

31

Teacup with Leaves, Kathleen Royster Lamb, 1996. Porcelainous stoneware. Glazed with B3A, (p.100), applied and partially wiped off. Fired to cone 10. 12.5 × 20 × 23cm (5 × 8 × 9in.). *Photo by the artist.*

a sponge to remove material provides very good control and allows you gradually to reveal the final surface.

Kathleen Royster Lamb develops complex surfaces that enhance her botanical forms by applying and wiping away a simple barium-rich glaze (B3A, see p.100). As she removes the glaze from the white stoneware, she reveals and expresses the form through new highlights and striated colour (see image above). Aurore Chabot works with commercially produced underglazes, copper washes and clay sigillatas in her richly aged surfaces. In *Tipping Points* she stains the piece with a layer of black copper oxide and wipes the surface to create a sense of age. She also applies a blue terra-sigillata slip to the two tips as well as various Amaco Velvet and Ceramichrome underglazes to develop stronger colour responses. After firing the pieces Aurore will modify the uni-form colour of the underglaze surfaces with additional layers of copper oxide applied and wiped off (see image p.29).

Layering dry glazes can be simple and quite easy. It just requires a bit more patience to conceive of the process requiring two or more glaze firings and the time to re-fire. Many artists achieve quite complex effects with only one or two glazes applied and fired in different ways. As the ceramic sculptor Scott Chamberlain observed in a letter, 'It must be said that I keep it very simple. That is, I use mostly one glaze and then if the surface needs more, I fire it again with something on top. I have been known to fire things up to 12 times to get the surface I want. I also pay close attention to thickness and thinness of glaze ... I sometimes use a very thick glaze and then after a firing where I get cracks and blistering, etc., glaze it again to temper the craggy surfaces.'

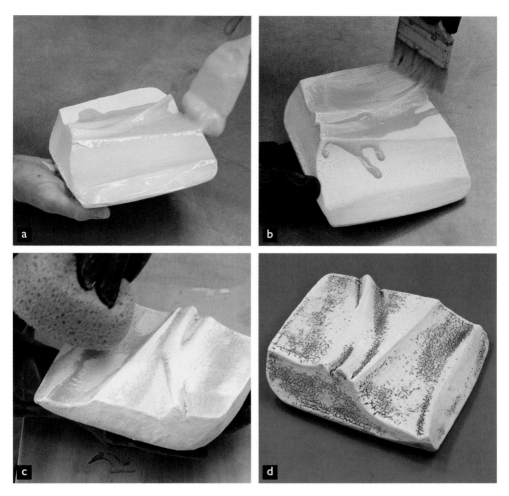

A coat of dry yellow base glaze (BL5, p.74) is applied and fired onto the piece to cone (a). A coating of copper wash (see tile CO2, p.130) is liberally applied (b), and then sponged off (c). The piece is re-fired to cone 04 (d). *Photos by the author.*

As the demonstration photographs show, developing a visually complex surface is often a case of layering a dark and a light surface, and wiping or sanding the surface to develop a greater sense of depth.

Most commonly, the recesses of a piece are emphasised by staining them with a coating of a dark slip or oxide or glaze, and then wiping away the surface. This coat may need to be fired on to avoid

smearing it – though in some cases it is fine to apply again right on top. The next layer may be a light coating of an engobe or a glaze, which will be stained by the oxide beneath and thus show a two-toned surface. Dark recesses enhance the sense of physical depth because they conform to our visual expectations of shadows in recessed areas and highlights on raised surfaces. In the images above copper wash is applied and wiped away, then a

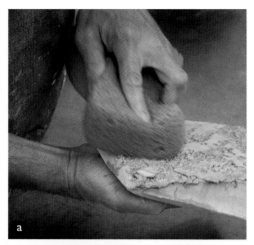

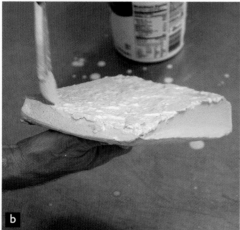

LEFT Copper wash (see tile CO2, p.130) is applied to a bisque-fired piece and then wiped off with a sponge (a). A coating of engobe (E16, p.52) is applied (b) and the piece is fired to cone 04 (c). This process also works well with coloured engobes applied quite thinly.

moderate layer of white engobe is applied. The firing causes the copper to stain the engobe, resulting in a surface with a natural variation of tonalities. In the images on the previous page, a slightly textured glaze (BL5A, p.74) was applied and fired onto the piece, then copper wash was applied and allowed to stain all the pits and fissures of the glaze. Wiping away the excess highlights both the form and the variation of the glaze surface.

Harris Deller is well-known for his strongly graphic black & white work, with black glaze inlaid into a white clay body. In a recent tile piece he layers a white terra-sigillata slip (E21, p.48) over a black sigillata, and incises through it, removing part of the surface layer before firing to cone 10 (see opposite). Lana Wilson achieves a similarly dramatic effect with her *Dry Blue Vase*, (p.27) applying the (E12, p.50) engobe coloured with 25% black copper oxide, and sponging off the surface to produce a high-contrast finish highlighting the richly detailed clay.

Layering also allows you to work with raw clay slips or very fragile surfaces by fusing them onto a more fused glaze underneath. In the images, a dark glaze has been applied to a tile and fired to maturity at cone 6. A thick layer of a high-shrinkage slip (E1A) is then applied and the piece is re-fired. During the drying and firing the slip shrinks and pulls away from the clay body, but when the glaze melts again the slip is fused into place, making it quite stable and durable (see also the tile set example, showing E1A over E10, on p.119).

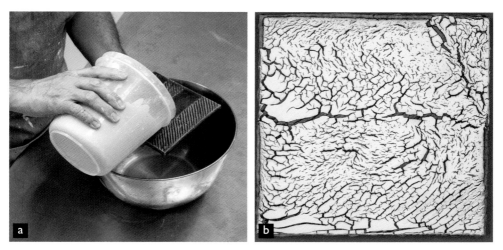

A tile has been glazed with B5A (see p.102) and fired to cone 6. A coating of white slip (E1A, p.118) is poured over it and allowed to dry (a). The tile is fired again to cone 6 (b). Variation in thickness of the glaze and in the tile surface influence the cracking pattern in this high-shrinkage slip. This works well with many base glazes.

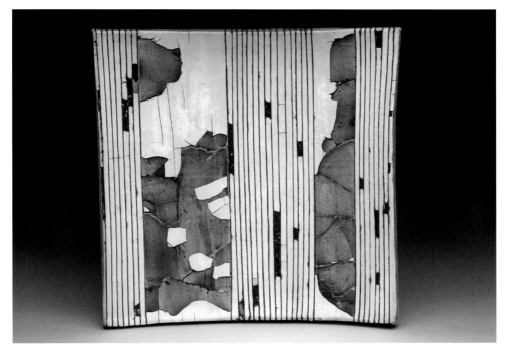

Harris Deller, *Wall Plate: Marking Time Series with 3 Bars*, 2003. White terra sigillata (E21, p.48) applied over black sigillata in varying thicknesses and incised through, fired to cone 10.33 × 33cm (13 × 13in.). *Photo by Jeff Bruce.*

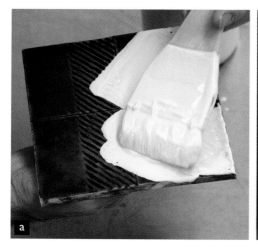 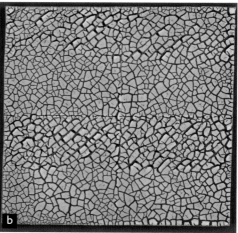

A tile is glazed with Lana's Purple Aqua (B7, p.106) (a) and fired to cone 04. A coating of crawl glaze (SE10, p.116) is brushed on thickly and the tile is re-fired to cone 04 (b).

A related technique is shown in the images above, in which a dry crawl-type glaze (SE10, p.116) is applied over a fired glaze (B7, p.106). In the subsequent firing the white crawl glaze is partially stained with the colour of the base glaze, the extent of the staining varying with the thickness of the glaze. This type of dry-on-wet layering can lend interesting highlights and drama to the surface. However, if the glaze is too glossy it may slide on vertical surfaces. One solution is to lower the final firing temperature by two cones or so, to the point where the slip is fused on but the glaze does not become fluid.

A crackle slip can also be effective as a base surface, as Mark Derby demonstrates in *Voyager* (see image p.61). Mark sprays slip (E30, p.52) on red earthenware bisque and fires it on to develop a peeling-paint surface. He then sprays on glaze (A12B, p.62) and re-fires. The high-shrinkage slip is fragile until it is fused on with the alkaline glaze, but contrast with the dark body and the chipped slip surface adds drama to his piece. On her sculpture *Primate* (see

image p. 67), Mikey Walsh reversed that process and used a thin coat of the semi-gloss glaze Tar Black (BL22, p.74) on the greenware form, bisque-fired it, and then applied a coat of red terra sigillata (E20, p.52) to it and fired it again. The sigillata fused to the glaze, matting and modifying it.

There are many other surface possibilities that haven't been mentioned, including applying and firing a crawl-type glaze (see chapter 9) and then applying another glaze over it and sanding or wiping off the excess. The second glaze will fill the cracks in between the crawl glaze and interact with it in various ways. In another interesting technique used by Andi Moran in *Implements* (see image opposite), a thick layer of ceramic stain is applied to the surface of a fired glaze (CO28, p.134) and re-fired to develop a crusty texture. Additional glaze is applied and the process repeated, building up quite textural surfaces. There are few limits to the possibilities that exist and may be discovered through enlightened experimentation with multiple glaze/slip/oxide applications and re-firings.

One concern associated with re-firing ceramic pieces is an increased risk of thermal shock to the clay body. This is highest typically in dense red earthenware or vitrified stoneware clay bodies, which may develop a higher quantity of crystobalite, a form of silica that goes through quartz inversion twice and as low as 226°C (439°F). Even low crystobalite bodies can crack upon re-firing if they are very dense and rapidly or unevenly heated. Solutions to this problem include shifting to a lower-iron clay body, which is more open and less mature at the glaze firing temperature. Moderately grogged stoneware clay bodies based on fireclay are quite versatile and will usually tolerate multiple firings up to cone 6 without difficulty. Perhaps the most effective way to control thermal shock is to carefully monitor the increase of heat during the firing. The availability and use of programmable kiln controllers has made this quite easy for electric kiln firings. For glaze firing I typically use a three-step programme that increases the heat by 83°C (150°F) an hour until 510°C (950°F), whereupon the rate of rise slows to 42°C (75°F) an hour until 649°C (1200°F), at which point it is safely past the point of quartz inversion. I then resume a rise of 83°C (150°F) or more an hour. If the work is particularly large I advance the temperature more slowly. Finally, even heating is helpful in avoiding thermal shock. Avoid stacking large platters or flat work tightly in small kilns. Keep pieces several inches away from kiln-element coils or burners, and allow adequate space around the work for heat to circulate in a uniform way.

Implement Series, Andi Moran, 2005. Glazed with CO28 (p.134) sponged on and off and fired. Green stain heavily applied and then more CO28. Fired to cone 04. 36 × 15 × 5cm (14 × 6 × 2in.). *Photo by Tom Joynt.*

Range Finding, Jeremy Jernegan, 1996. Ceramic and steel. Tile elements are monoprinted with Amaco Velvet underglazes fired to cone 3; the chain is glazed with copper wash and E16 (p.52) and fired to cone 04. 183 × 71 × 15cm (72 × 28 × 6in.). *Photo by the artist.*

Chapter 4
Slips and engobes

Clay slips

Slips and engobes are the driest end of the clay-to-glaze continuum, but provide many opportunities for developing rich and repeatable surfaces. A slip is essentially a clay or clay-body formula mixed with water to a fluid consistency. It may be the very same body as the piece is built from, or one which has strongly contrasting qualities, like a porcelain clay body applied to stoneware. Slips are very useful for developing surface texture on pieces, as well as covering and changing the appearance of the body. Slips normally have a high ratio of raw clay, which causes them to shrink significantly as they dry and fire. Because of this, slips are most commonly applied to leatherhard clay, which shrinks along with them and ensures a stable bond. Slips can be formulated with significant amounts of flux to fire to a vitrified, almost glassy surface, or they may be mostly clay and quite matt. At earthenware temperatures most slips are dry when fired. The slip's shrinkage can cause the coating to delaminate and flake off a bisque-fired body, particularly if the coat is fairly thick.

That said, there are quite a few artists who use thin layers of slips on bisque ware to good effect. Kaolin-rich slips have become very popular for atmospheric firings like wood or salt/soda firings. The slip coat is usually applied very thinly, bisque ware being dipped in a watery mix so as to just coat and colour the ware. Kaolins like EPK, Grolleg or Avery provide a near-white surface with a small amount of iron that can develop shades of orange or brown under the influence of sodium vapour in a reduction atmosphere.

Many so-called 'crackle slips' are simply high-kaolin or ball-clay formulas that have significant shrinkage and crack dramatically when applied to bisque ware (see also Chapter 9). The problem with this kind of effect is the slip

Look Ahead Teapot #7, Barbara Frey, 2002. Coloured porcelain slips and inlaid bits of coloured porcelain. Fired to cone 6. 15 × 15 × 18cm (6 × 6 × 7in.). *Photo by Harrison Evans.*

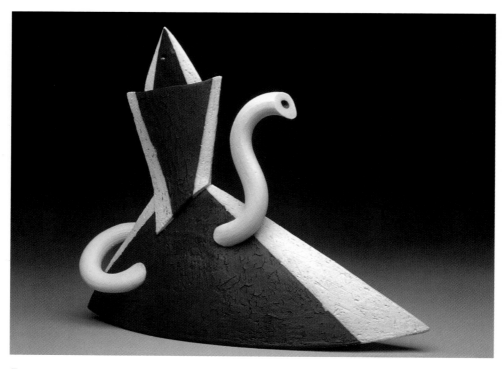

Teapot with Passive Spout (Suppressed Volume Series Black on White) Harris Deller, 2005. Black and white terra sigillata, fired to cone 10 (E21, p.48). 25 × 23 × 7.5cm (10 × 9 × 3in.). *Photo by the artist.*

may delaminate after the firing when the piece is handled. The high clay content of such a slip means it also has very high alumina content, particularly in the case of kaolins. The alumina ensures there is little if any fusion between the body and the glaze, resulting in a fragile crust. Vapour glazing or fly ash in a wood kiln helps to fuse the cracking slip onto the surface, making it more practical and less risky. High-clay-content slips may also be used on top of a fired glaze as a final layer (see Chapter 3). Slips can also be coloured with raw metal oxides like iron, cobalt and manganese, as well as prepared ceramic stains.

Because the degree of fusion in a slip tends to be low and the alumina content high, the resulting colour responses tend to be fairly pastel and uniform unless the metallic colourant content is high.

Terra sigillata

Terra sigillata is essentially a pure clay slip with extremely fine particle size. It normally contains no flux or filler and tends to be fairly opaque and refractory, but has a smooth, almost glossy surface. True sigillata has a remarkable feel and for many artists suggests the surface of still-damp clay.

Historically, sigillatas were used by Greek potters to create the refined and finely painted black and red Attic wares. The surfaces were burnished to develop a gloss, but there was no glass formed at the low temperatures at which they were

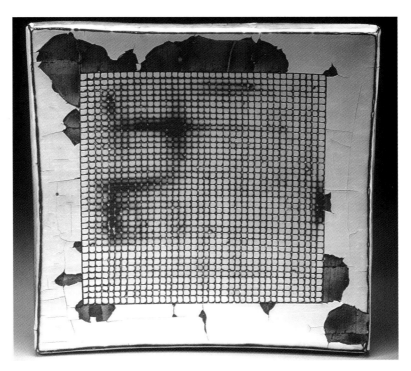

Wall Plate: Grid Series, Harris Deller, 1999. White terra sigillata (E21, p.48) applied over black sigillata in varying thicknesses and incised through, fired to cone 10. 33 × 33cm (13 × 13in.). *Photo by Jeff Bruce.*

fired. Black Attic ware was achieved through heavy reduction late in the firing, which charged the slip with carbon. Terra sigillata may be made with any clay, and will exhibit the colour associated with the clay. For instance, iron red results from earthenwares, creamy whites come from ball clay, and brighter whites from kaolins. The burnished gloss of a sigillata is best preserved when fired to earthenware temperatures, but it may also be fired to cone 6 or higher. Some sigillatas are coloured with stains or oxides, but additions of more than 10% can interfere with the unique character of the surface.

The usual procedure for making sigillata involves a levigation, or settling process. The dry clay powder is vigorously mixed with a specific quantity of water, usually with a small amount of an alkaline deflocculant like soda ash to help it remain suspended longer. Some formulas call for ball-milling the slip at this point. The mix is allowed to settle for one to six days while the larger clay particles separate from the finer. The upper layer is carefully removed and used, and the rest is discarded. Mikey Walsh gives the following directions for her 'sig' (sigillata) (E20, p.52): 'Ball-mill all ingredients for 4 hours. Pour mix into large glass jar or see-through plastic container. Let sit for 1 week. Using a turkey baster, siphon off and discard the clear portion of water at the top. Then remove the next layer of the opaque unsettled portion (about 3 cups). This is

Siamese Split Open, Aurore Chabot, 2001. Amaco Velvet underglazes and copper oxide wash. Black terra sigillata on exterior. Fired to cone 04. 27 × 23 × 15cm (10½ × 9 × 6in.). *Photo by the artist.*

oxide stains or other glazes as one would an underglaze.

Engobes

Engobes are similar to slips, and in some cases the words are used interchangeably. I maintain the slightly old-fashioned use of the term to refer to a low-shrinkage slip which has a greater amount of fusion when fired, also known as a vitreous engobe. The term engobe comes from the French, and has generally meant to coat or cover (with slip). The etymology is said to be the words *en* + *gober*, meaning to gulp or swallow whole,[7] which provides a graphic way to remember it. Vitreous slip, vitreous engobe and underglaze are all names for essentially the same thing.

I find the use of engobes to be one of the most versatile and controllable techniques to develop a dry surface on any bisque-fired ceramic work. They are an excellent way to modify a surface with a high degree of confidence in the outcome. They tend to produce uniform colour and texture, but are well suited to layered application and repeated firings to achieve varied and complex results. By themselves fired engobes are pretty uniform, and rarely create a dramatic surface. In fact, I use them at times to cover up or quieten down an area of a piece that is too busy or too visually active. Their predictable and uniform nature is a real asset in those applications. However, one can layer engobes over metallic oxides and achieve some quite active and varied surfaces. My personal favorite for earthenware temperatures is to use a copper wash and an earthenware engobe (see Chapter 3).

An engobe is essentially a clay-based slip with a significant amount of glaze material added to it. The criteria for a

your yield of 'pure' terra sig.'

Harris Deller has a simpler process for his grolleg sigillata with no deflocculant (E21, p.48): 'Mix thoroughly. Allow to settle for 3–4 days, then decant the water on top. Allow to settle for another 3–4 days, then decant the watery bit on top. Allow to settle for another 3 days and decant the thin slip on top and discard. Carefully pour off the middle "half and half" consistency slip for the sigillata. Discard the rest.'

Typically, a thin coating is applied to either leatherhard ware or bisque. After this has dried slightly, the sigillata is normally burnished with the hand or a cloth to develop a shine. Sigillata coatings may be layered with metal

normal engobe are that it may be applied to bisque ware without excessive shrinkage, and that it be quite fused but not glossy at its maturing temperature. Engobes may be coloured with opacifiers like tin or zirconium to make them very white, or metallic oxides like cobalt, or prepared ceramic stains. Because engobes are typically very high in alumina, they tend to produce rather dark and drab colours with most metallic oxides. Strongly coloured engobes intended primarily for decorating are often referred to as underglazes. These are usually well ground or ball-milled to produce a very uniform colour and surface. Because they are so uniform, they can be diluted with a large amount of water to produce delicate and subtle tints on bisque ware. There are a number of good manufactured underglazes available, particularly for the low to medium temperature range of cone 06–cone 6. Many artists use these almost like paint, for their predictable and strong colour responses, employing them in combination with other techniques.

Using commercially prepared ceramic stains such as the Mason or Degussa brands, you can make brightly coloured engobes similar to those that are com-mercially prepared, but for much lower cost. Stains produce a stable, predictable colour and potentially a very wide range of hues. Most commercially produced ceramic stains are quite stable and will work well in most engobe formulas. However, some colours do require certain ranges of chemical compositions to develop their full colour. For example, the chrome-tin pinks and crimsons need some calcium in the formula and cannot tolerate zinc oxide. Testing the colours is the best approach, and stain manufac-turers will provide recommendations for

Waterman Point, Jeremy Jernegan, 1994. Ceramic and steel. Glazed with copper wash sponged off, E16 (p.52) applied and fired to cone 04. 226 × 46 × 25cm (89 × 18 × 10in.). *Photo by the artist.*

43

their stains. An engobe formulated with adequate calcium, such as E16, works well for a wide spectrum of ceramic stain-based colours at earthenware temperatures. Typically 10–20% ceramic stain is added to an engobe to produce dense colour. Most stains also work well at high temperature but require a different engobe base such as E3A.

The key parameters of an engobe are the ratio of clay to non-clay (which controls shrinkage), and the selection of fluxing materials to develop fusion. A good way to visualise the relationships between glaze, engobe and slip is to look at the ratio between the silica and the alumina in each. In most glazes silica is the glass former and alumina is the stiffener, giving it viscosity. A little alumina goes a long way in glaze, even at high temperatures. The usual source of alumina in a glaze or a slip is clay. We can compare the glaze formula for a smooth glossy cone 10 glaze called Refrigerator White, with that of a vitreous engobe, Engobe 'F' (E3A), and that of a conventional porcelain slip, TU White Slip (E1). It is easy to see in their formulas the clear trend from low clay content in the glaze (20%) to higher clay content in the slip (59.1%). Comparing the ratio of silica to alumina shows the relatively high ratio typical in a glaze and the low ratio found in a clay slip. The more alumina there is relative to silica, the drier and more refractory the

result will be. The ratios would be even more different if we were to compare earthenware glazes to slips.

The quantity and type of clay in the formula is important in assuring the engobe will both apply well and stay on a bisque-fired body. There is surprisingly wide latitude in the percentage of raw clay that will work, but generally speaking it should be less than 50% of the formula weight. Kaolins shrink less than ball clays and are typically whiter, so they are generally favoured. An easy way to reduce a shrinkage problem with the raw clay component in an engobe formula is to substitute calcined clay for part of it. To calcine simply means to fire a material, usually to low bisque temperature (cone 010–06). When a dry powdered clay is calcined, it is chemically the same, but no longer behaves as a raw clay when wetted, eliminating all plasticity and most shrinkage characteristics. This is helpful whenever one wants the chemical contributions of a large quantity of clay in the formula (principally the alumina) but not the physical characteristics. Calcined kaolin is commonly sold, but is also easily produced: simply fill a bisque-fired bowl with dry kaolin and bisque-fire it in the kiln along with other ware. If the kaolin is a bit lumpy, dry-screen it through a 30-mesh sieve before using.

	Refrigerator White	Engobe F	TU White Slip
G200 Feldspar	30	31.6	24.6
Whiting	20	0	0
Silica	30	27.3	14.8
Ball clay	20	9.5	24.6
EP Kaolin	0	31.6	34.5
Borax	0	0	1.5
Ratio of silica to alumina: 10.39 to 1		5.97 to 1	4.52 to 1

Engobes usually have very wide firing latitude (satisfactory results over 5 or more cones). Typically, engobes are optimised for either earthenware (cone 010–cone 1) or stoneware (cone 4–10) temperatures. They are not usually affected much by firing atmosphere, unless they contain large amounts of metallic oxides or glaze stains. While the expectation of an engobe is that it is 'fused' at its maturing temperature, there is wide interpretation as to what that means. Provided that a given formula is physically satisfactory in staying put on one's bisque ware and not shrinking off, how fused it is becomes a matter of taste, relative to the need for a durable surface. As the fluxing constituents of an engobe formula increase, the fired result becomes harder and less susceptible to scratching, but also somewhat less opaque and often less white.

Common materials for slips and engobes

Kaolin clays

These are considered primary clays in the sense that they occur close to where they form geologically, and they are also relatively pure, being free from iron and other contamination. Kaolins are fairly widespread and vary some-what from one source to another, although all of them are very refractory and fire to a near-white colour. The EPK is a popular Florida kaolin that is much cheaper than, but not as white or plastic as, the English Grolleg kaolin. Avery kaolin is favoured by some for the orange colour it develops in soda firings. Kaolins are the building blocks for high-temperature slips and engobes, providing a light-coloured, refractory base with moderate shrinkage.

Freak Hydra: Cross Section, Bonita Day, 1999. Glazed with copper wash applied and wiped off, coloured E16 engobes and finally E16 (p.52) in white. 64 × 36 × 41cm (25 × 14 × 16in.). *Photo by the author.*

Ball clays

These are described as secondary clays because they have been moved from their geological source and are slightly less pure, but have a very small particle size. There are many regional varieties, with the Kentucky OM-4 clay being a popular choice. Ball clays are highly plastic and exhibit significant shrinkage on drying. They bond well to clay bodies, have good green strength when dry, and work well in slips applied to leatherhard ware. They are relatively refractory and are used at both stoneware and earthenware temperatures.

Earthenware clays

These are primarily red earthenwares, naturally iron-rich secondary clays that are found in great quantities around the world. They vary considerably from mine to mine, but most have a mixed particle size and are only moderately plastic. Red Art, Ocmulgee and Newman Red are popular choices. The high iron content gives them a strong orange/red colour when fired and is also responsible for lowering their maturing temperature. Most red earthenwares mature at about cone 04 and will melt into a stiff brown glaze at cone 10. These clays are used for making iron-rich terra-sigillata slips, and are found in formulas for dark-coloured vitreous engobes. In addition to being the basis for an earthenware slip, they are a convenient and inexpensive way to add iron to any slip or engobe.

Slip clays

These are also secondary clays from riverbed areas, containing considerable amounts of metallic oxides such as iron and manganese resulting in a dark-brown or black slip colour and a fairly low maturing temperature. Commonly used slip clays include Albany (which is no longer available), Alberta, Barnard and Blackbird. Slip clays are commonly used for developing iron-rich stoneware glazes, but are also useful in dark slips and vitreous engobes.

Other clays

Fireclays are not common in most slips, but may be introduced for a warm colour or to develop a textural slip. Saggar clays or stoneware clays may likewise be used for variety, and all clays may be useful for making a terra sigillata. Grog (ground firebrick) may be added for texture, and molochite (very fine kaolin-based grog) may be used for texture and to reduce shrinkage in a porcelain slip. Similarly, fired or calcined kaolin is very helpful in reducing the drying and firing shrinkage of an engobe.

Feldspars

Most commonly potassium-rich spars, such as Custer or G-200, are used as the primary fluxing agent, making up 20–40% of a high-temperature slip or engobe. Feldspars contain silica, alumina and flux, and have wide firing latitude which makes them versatile and useful for almost all firing temperatures, though they must be supplemented with more active fluxes at low temperatures.

Silica

Ground flint is found in many stoneware slips and engobes, and some at earthenware temperatures as well. Silica is the primary glass former in a glaze and also aids vitrification in an engobe and slip. Silica is quite refractory, so its use at low temperatures tends to dry out a slip unless there is a considerable amount of flux in the formula. Like feldspar, silica does not shrink upon drying, so it is helpful in developing engobes that can be applied to bisque ware.

Glaze frits

These are available in a wide variety of formulas, and are very useful in fluxing

Eva, Barbara Frey, 2008. Red porcelain slip (coloured with US Pigment inclusion stain 1351) on leatherhard clay. Top section dipped in MC50 (p.86) with rust and glass chips sprinkled on. Fired to cone 6. 23 × 20 × 20 cm (9 × 8 × 8 in.) *Photo by Harrison Evans.*

a slip or engobe, particularly at earthenware temperatures. Ferro 3124 and 3134 supply calcium and boric oxide and are widely used. Frits are relatively expensive and tend to have a fairly strong melting action and a narrower range, so they are typically used in modest proportions (5–20%).

Other fluxing materials

Materials such as talc, whiting, gerstley borate and borax may be found as fluxing agents in slips and engobes. Borax acts as a deflocculant and hardens the surface of the dried slip.

Toxicity and health concerns

Low risk: Slips and engobes are some of the safest and least hazardous ceramic coatings one can use. Because they are primarily composed of clay, silica and feldspar, there is rarely a toxicity hazard (though some frits or colouring oxides may be hazardous if present in large quantities). When worked with as wet materials they are quite inert. However, silica dust inhalation is a concern when one is mixing, sanding or cleaning up dry slip or engobe residue.

Formulas for slip and engobe (E) tile set 1

E1: TU White Slip (J. Jernegan) – cone 10R		E4: Engobe G (J. Jernegan) – cone 10R		E3A: Engobe F (J. Jernegan) – cone 10R	
EPKaolin	34.7	EPKaolin	15.6	EPKaolin	31.6
Ball clay	24.7	Ball clay	6.2	Ball clay	9.4
Silica	14.9	Calcined kaolin	20.3	Silica	27.4
Potash spar	24.7	Silica	26.6	Custer spar	31.6
Borax	1.0	Custer spar	31.3		100
	100		100		
Zircopax	10	Borax	2	Borax	2

E3A1: Engobe F, red-brown – cone 10R		E3C: Engobe F, cool blue – cone 10R		E3D: Engobe F, black – cone 10R	
				EPKaolin	31.6
EPKaolin	31.6	EPKaolin	31.6	Ball clay	9.4
Ball clay	9.4	Ball clay	9.4	Silica	27.4
Silica	27.4	Silica	27.4	Custer spar	31.6
Custer spar	31.6	Custer spar	31.6		100
	100		100		
Borax	2	Borax	2	Borax	2
Copper carb.	4	Copper carb.	3	Manganese dioxide	4
Red iron oxide	1	Cobalt carb.	1	Black iron oxide	5
				Cobalt carb.	2

E3A over CO2 (toxic) – cone 10R		E3A over CO4 – cone 10R		E8: Mottled Engobe – cone 10R	
CO2: Copper Carbonate Wash		*CO4: Red Iron Oxide Wash*			
Copper carbonate	100 g	Red iron oxide	50 g	Calcined kaolin	34
Water	2 cups	Rutile	50 g	EPKaolin	6
Add CMC gum as needed to aid in suspension.		Gerstley borate	15 g	Potash spar	19
		Nepheline syenite	15 g	Silica	15
		Water	2 cups	Whiting	21
		Add CMC gum as needed to aid in suspension.		Nepheline syenite	3
				Bentonite	2
					100

E21: Grolleg Sigillata (H. Deller) – cone 10R		E7: Hint of Sheen – cone 10R		E6: Textural Brown (J. Jernegan) – cone 10R	
Grolleg kaolin	10,000 g	Goldart	46.4	Fireclay	46
Water	4 gal.	Ball clay	6.9	Ball clay	21
		Custer spar	6.7	Custer	17
		Cornwall stone	32.8	Fine grog	6
		Whiting	5.6	Whiting	3
		Nepheline syenite	1.6	EPKaolin	2
			100	Silica	5
See Chapter 3 for mixing sigillatas.					100

Slip and engobe (E) tile set 1 (*see formulas opposite*)

Formulas for slip and engobe (E) tile set 2

E25: Base Engobe (V. Cushing) – cone 10R		E5: Engobe G-2 (J. Jernegan) – cone 10R		E9: Salt Engobe, Yellow-Tan – cone 10R	
EPKaolin	30	EPKaolin	25	EPKaolin	30
OM–4 ball clay	30	Ball clay	10	Ball clay	10
Nepheline syenite	15	Silica	25	Silica	30
Silica	15	Custer spar	40	Nepheline syenite	30
Zircopax	10		100		100
	100				
		Borax	1	Rutile	6
Chromium oxide	4	Black stain	25		

E22A: TU Metallic Slip – cone 10R		E24: Titanium Yellow Slip – cone 10R		E2: Slip 2750 (P. Horsley) – cone 6	
EPKaolin	27.7	Nepheline syenite	31.6	Grolleg kaolin	30
Ball clay	19.5	OM-4 ball clay	63.2	C and C clay	30
Silica	12.2	Silica	5.2	6-Tile kaolin	10
G200 spar	20.3		100	Nepheline syenite	15
Zircopax	20.3			Silica 200M	15
	100	Tin oxide	5		100
		Titanium dioxide	10		
Borax	1			Bentonite	2
Black iron oxide	12			Copper carb.	8

E4; Engobe G (J. Jernegan) – cone 6		E11: Conrad Black Engobe (J. Conrad) – cone 6		E28: Fake Avery Flashing Slip (R. Burkett) – cone 10R	
		Borax	5		
EPKaolin	15.6	Whiting	5	Nepheline syenite	25
Ball clay	6.2	Nepheline syenite	10	EPKaolin	42
Calcined kaolin	20.3	Potash spar	15	Calcined kaolin	30
Silica	26.6	EPKaolin	20	Red Horse clay	3
Custer spar	31.3	Ball clay	20		100
	100	Silica	25		
Borax	2		100	Darvan	811
		Mason Stain 6600	10		

E27: Black Slip (A. Moran) – cone 04 (toxic)		E13: Black Chalks (J. Jernegan) – cone 1 (toxic)		E12: Dry Borax Engobe (L. Wilson) – cone 6	
Redart clay	46.7	Bentonite	20	Kaolin	57
OM-4 ball clay	23.4	Pemco lead frit PB 742	10	Silica	29
Manganese dioxide	14	Black Mason Stain 6600	70	Borax	14
Black stain	11.2		100		100
Black iron oxide	4.7	Dry screen then mix with water until mix is sticky but stiff; roll coils to desired size and allow them to dry.		Rutile	25
	100				

Slip and engobe (E) tile set 2 (*see formulas opposite*)

Formulas for slip and engobe (E) tile set 3

E20: Red Terra Sigillata (M. Walsh) – cone 04	E21: Grolleg Sigillata (H. Deller) – cone 04	E19: White Terra Sigillata (M. Walsh) – cone 04
Redart clay 1400 g Red iron oxide 50 g Hot water 14 cups (3.3 l) Soda ash 45 g	Grolleg kaolin 10,000 g Water 4 gal. (15.1 l)	Ball clay 1,500 g Water 14 cups (3.3 l) Soda ash 45 g
See Chapter 3 for mixing sigillatas.	See Chapter 3 for mixing sigillatas.	See Chapter 3 for mixing sigillatas.

E31: Black Sigillata (A. Chabot) – cone 04 (toxic)	E14: Low Fire Slip (S. Stephenson) – cone 04	E26: SDSU Vitreous Engobe – cone 06
Carbondale red clay 1500 g Deflocculant (Darvan #7) 7 g Water 14 cups (3.3 l) After settling, add the following to 3 cups sigillata: Cobalt carb. 32 g Black Mason stain 83 g Black copper oxide 187 g See Chapter 3 for mixing sigillatas.	EPKaolin 12.5 Tile 6 kaolin 12.5 Ball clay 25 Frit 3124 20 Talc 5 Silica 20 Pyrophilite 5 ‾‾‾‾ 100 Zircopax 5	OM-4 ball clay 20 Silica 30 Frit 3110 30 Talc 5 Borax 5 Zircopax 10 ‾‾‾‾ 100

E16: Class Engobe (J. Jernegan) – cone 04	E16 over CO2 – cone 04	E30: Derby Crawl – cone 06
Calcined kaolin 10.5 Ball clay 15.8 Bentonite 5.3 Wollastonite 15.8 Potash spar 31.6 Frit 3124 21 ‾‾‾‾ 100 Zircopax 10	*CO2: Copper Carbonate Wash (toxic)* Copper carb. 100 g Water 2 cups (0.48 l) Add CMC gum as needed to aid in suspension.	Soda ash 14 Dolomite 3 EPKaolin 69 Magnesium carb. 14 ‾‾‾‾ 100

E33: Chinese Green (from L. Duryea) – cone 04	E29: Engobe Base for mono-printing (J. Jernegan) – cone 04	E17: Engobe Variant for Stains (J. Jernegan) – cone 06
OM-4 ball clay 25 EPKaolin 25 Nepheline syenite 13 Gerstley borate 12 Silica 25 Lithium carb. 5 ‾‾‾‾ 100 Copper carb. 3	Frit P-54 28.6 Nepheline syenite 22.9 EPKaolin 11.4 Ball clay 11.4 Bentonite 8.6 Mason Stain (dark teal blue) 17.1 ‾‾‾‾ 100	Bentonite 5 Wollastonite 15 Potash spar 25 Frit 3124 27 Calcined kaolin 12 Mason Stain 6006 16 ‾‾‾‾ 100

Slip and engobe (E) tile set 3 (*see formulas opposite*)

Ironside, Mark Derby, 2001. Glazed with E30 (p.52) crackle slip under A12A (p.62). Fired at cone 04. 28 × 33 × 10cm (11 × 13 × 4in.). *Photo by Katherine Slingluff.*

Chapter 5

Alkaline glazes: rich in sodium, potassium and lithium

The alkalis are often grouped together in glaze chemistry because they have similar formula structures – namely, Na_2O (sodium), K_2O (potassium) and Li_2O (lithium) – which make them bases, the chemical opposite of acids. (If the pH of a compound is greater than 7 it is described as basic (a base), if it is less than 7 it is described as acidic (an acid). 'Base' in this context is a specific chemistry term.) Alkalis also share some general characteristics in their influence on glazes. Each of the three is quite powerful as a fluxing agent, which means that a relatively small quantity can produce a significant melting action at a given temperature. Because of this they are both useful and common in low-temperature glazes, and are also used in stoneware glazes, but in lower quantities. Perhaps the most familiar example of an alkaline-rich glaze is a brilliant turquoise-blue earthenware glaze, such as those found on Persian tiles.

Alkalis are relatively inexpensive and occur naturally in a large number of forms. They are sometimes introduced in relatively pure and highly soluble forms, as in the case of carbonates such as sodium carbonate (Na_2CO_3) or lithium carbonate (Li_2CO_3). Soluble compounds have traditionally been a problem for potters, because of their tendency to migrate through the ware when drying and cause unexpected and varied results. However, that sort of spontaneous variation is appreciated by artists seeking unusual surfaces that appear mottled and organic. Sodium carbonate, for instance, can produce textured and quite unpredictable glaze surfaces. Sodium will also volatilise (turn to a gas) quite readily during the firing, and may affect unglazed clay nearby.

Ghost, Mikey Walsh, 2006. Glazed with A17 (p.62) over thick white slip. Fired to cone 04. 46 × 30.5 × 11.5cm (18 × 12 × 4½in.). *Photo by Kevin Duffy.*

One Time Stack, Jeremy Jernegan, 1990. Glazed with A3 (p.64) in varied thicknesses. Fired to cone 04. 84 × 53 × 61cm (33 × 21 × 24in.). *Photo by the artist.*

Matt glazes rich in raw soluble alkalis include flux-saturated type and partially melted matts. These glazes are some of the most unpredictable and, if they get wet, may leach alkalis out of the surface even months after the firing. The soluble alkalis can also be troublesome in the glaze bucket, as they deflocculate the glaze slop, and in high concentrations evaporation causes them to migrate up the side, growing crystals that can be difficult to get back into solution. Results with such glazes can vary noticeably between how they look when applied after they are first mixed, versus how they look when applied days or weeks later. In very high quantities they can solidify into a hard mass after being mixed with water. For these reasons some artists mix only small batches of highly soluble glazes and use them promptly, discarding or recycling them after a week or so.

Alkalis are commonly introduced in a relatively insoluble form as feldspars, which can be thought of as naturally occurring frits. With the exception of Cornwall stone, most feldspars fall into the broad categories of sodium-, potassium- or lithium-rich. The concentrations of alkali in feldspars are much lower than in the relatively pure carbonate form, and consequently their behaviour is considerably less dramatic. Introduced as feldspars they may be one constituent of all types of matt glazes, depending on the other ingredients and the firing temperature. Though sodium and potassium are quite similar in much of their behaviour, they are not usually substituted for each other. In fact, in glaze formulas feldspars are often simply designated as a 'soda spar' or 'potash spar', indicating that the particular named feldspar is not as important as whether sodium or potassium is the dominant fluxing oxide.

Frank Sundstrum, *Just Another Teapot*, 2008. Glazed with A22 (p.62) applied over black clay body. Fired at cone 04. 23 × 6.5 × 18cm (9 × 2.5 × 7in.). *Photo by R. Burkett.*

Colour responses

Alkalis have quite a strong effect on bright colour development, most notably in producing brilliant turquoise from copper at low temperature. This is especially true of lithium, which promotes rich turquoise blues from copper even in sintered matt-type glazes and even with quite small percentages of lithium present (see tiles A3 and A20A, p.64) Chromium will produce a bright yellow-green in sodium-rich glazes (see tiles A22 and A12, p.62), while iron tends toward blue and cobalt tends toward pink.[8]

Nesting Pink Succulent, Lisa Conway, 2005. Commercial glazes multilayered on interior, A20 (p.62) on exterior. Fired to cone 04. 46 × 61 × 46cm (18 × 24 × 18in.). *Photo by Grace Weston.*

Melting point and coefficient of expansion

Sodium has a melting point of 900°C (1652°F), potassium 700°C (1291°F), and lithium 800°C (1472°F).[9] Of the alkalis, lithium is the most powerful melting agent, but they are all very active. Particularly distinctive are the differences in how much each one expands upon heating and contracts on cooling, a phenomenon known as the coefficient of expansion. Every element has a different rate of expansion, and a glaze rich in a particular oxide will share those characteristics. Sodium, for instance, has the highest coefficient of expansion of the three, and the highest of any common glaze flux. Potassium is also very high, but slightly less than sodium. Lithium, however, has a much lower coefficient of expansion, less than a third of the coefficient of sodium.[10]

This characteristic is important, as it relates to the fit of the glaze with the clay body beneath it. At the height of the firing, when the glaze is a liquid glass (or even a partially liquid glass in the case of matt glazes), it matches the size of the clay body it is fused to. As the clay and glaze both cool, the amount by which each shrinks is often not the same. Sodium- or potassium-rich earthenware glazes typically show considerable 'crazing' because they shrink so much more than the clay body they have been applied to; the cracking results from the tension or pulling-apart of the glaze as it cools. Conversely, earthenware glazes very high in lithium may not shrink enough to fit the cooled body. In moderation this phenomenon, in which the glaze is said to be 'in compression', is a good thing; however, under excessive compression the glaze may show signs of 'shivering', as slivers of the hardened glaze pop off the body that is shrinking underneath it. Lithium can be seen as a complement to sodium in moderating the extremes of glaze fit.

These discrepancies of clay and glaze shrinkage are less likely to be a problem in matt glazes than in glossy glazes. In part this is because craze lines show less in opaque glazes, and issues of utility are less of a concern in sculptural applications. Sintered matts are also less well bonded to the clay and may accommodate more tension and compression than fully melted glazes. That said, extreme and unorthodox glaze formulations with alkaline glaze can cause problems with glaze fit.

Common sources of alkalis in glaze formulas

Sodium

Sodium carbonate (Na_2CO_3), or soda ash, sodium bicarbonate ($NaHCO_3$), or baking soda, and sodium chloride ($NaCl$), or table salt, are sources of pure sodium and are all very powerful fluxes; they are also very soluble, and absorb moisture from the air, causing caking and clumping. Soda ash is a caustic base. Sodium chloride and sodium bicarbonate are not commonly used in glazes, but both are introduced in salt and soda firings.

Borax ($Na_2O_2B_2O_3 10H_2O$) is a source of sodium and boron together. It is a very powerful flux, and also very soluble and caustic, readily absorbing moisture from the air. Borax is used in raku glazes and other speciality earthenware glazes because it melts readily and will form a pseudo-glass all by itself. The granular nature of borax contributes to spotting and speckling in some glazes, particularly dry sintered matts. It is better not to grind this type of glaze to a powder or to screen it too finely. Some artists sprinkle powdered borax on top of a damp glaze or slip surface to promote speckling.

Tissue: Structure for Replicating Matter, Bonita Day, 1999. Glazed with coloured engobes (E16, p.52) with copper applied and wiped off. Overall coat of A3 (p.64). Fired to cone 04. 127 × 356 × 56cm (50 × 140 × 22in.). *Photo by the author.*

Soda feldspars have many types, but common brands or types include Minspar, Kona F-4, NC-4 and nepheline syenite. These feldspars are a common source of sodium for high-temperature glazes and natural frits, limiting the solubility of sodium to very low levels. Nepheline syenite is somewhat more active than other soda spars and is found in higher percentages in mid-range and low-temperature clays and glazes. Sodium is quite widespread, and many types of feldspar contain small amounts of sodium even if it is not the primary flux mentioned.

Sodium-rich frits are physically, a mixture of raw glaze materials melted together in a crucible, and then poured into water to chill and shatter. The resulting glass granules are washed and ground to a fine powder. Chemically, frits may have any formula desired and are similar to complete glazes though they are not usually intended to be used by themselves. Frits are relatively expensive, but they are reliable and provide an easy way to introduce sodium or other soluble oxides in an insoluble form. Depending on their formula they may be either very active or only moderately so. Most contain other fluxes as well as alumina and silica. Frits are manufactured in many formulations by four or five major manufacturers. Sodium-rich frits include Ferro 3110, 3269, 3264 and 3288. The formulas for most frits are available from distributors, printed texts and online references like Digitalfire.com. Many popular frit formulas may be found in similar and exactly equivalent frits in other manufacturers' product lines.

Cryolite (Na_3AlF_6) is a naturally insoluble source of sodium and alumina. It is quite an active flux, but not widely used because of the fluorine gas that is liberated during the firing (see Chapter 9) In high quantities it may also cause opacity.

Potassium

Potassium carbonate (K_2CO_3), or pearl ash, is pure potassium, and like soda ash is very soluble and a powerful flux. It readily absorbs moisture from the air, has a granular nature and tends to clump readily. Pearl ash is a caustic base.

Potassium-rich feldspars are a common way to introduce potassium in a non-soluble form. Common brands include Custer, G-200 and K-200. These are relatively low-activity fluxes, but very important in mid- and high-temperature glazes, where they may make up 30–40% of the glaze. They are also widely used as fluxes in stoneware and porcelain clay bodies, as well as in slips and engobes. They are inexpensive, non-toxic and have a fairly wide firing range. Potash spars often contain significant quantities of sodium as well.

Lithium

Lithium carbonate (Li_2CO_3) is a pure and somewhat soluble source of lithium, and acts as a powerful flux. It is the most common way to introduce lithium into glazes. The crystalline nature of this material promotes specking and surface variation in dry glazes.

Lithium-rich feldspars are an insoluble source of lithium in lower concentrations, allowing for common use in high-temperature glazes. They are much less active fluxes than lithium carbonate. Petalite and spodumene are quite pure, containing just lithium, alumina and silica, with spodumene having the higher concentration of lithium. Lepidolite is the third lithium spar, which also contains potassium and small amounts of sodium.

Voyager, Mark Derby, 2006. Glazed with E30 (p.52) crackle slip under A12B (p.62), fired at cone 04. 28 × 33 × 10cm (11 × 13 × 4in.). *Photo by Katherine Slingluff.*

Toxicity and health concerns

Moderate risk: Sodium and potassium compounds are not considered an acute toxicity hazard; however, lithium is. All dusts should be managed so as to avoid inhalation, to reduce chronic respiration hazards and irritation due to the interaction of caustic materials with respiratory membranes. In their soluble forms, all the alkalis are caustic and can cause serious irritation to skin due to their high pH values. Care should be taken to protect skin and to avoid inhaling dusts. Because of the volatility of sodium, good ventilation is particularly important when firing.

A4: Lithium Slip Glaze – cone 06 (toxic)		A11: Crusty Olive – cone 06		A22: Green Moss C (L. Wilson/ F. Sundstrom) – cone 06 (toxic)	
Lithium carb.	27.7	Borax	20		
EPKaolin	13.9	Sodium carb.	20	Lithium carb.	80
Silica	55.5	Nepheline syenite	26.6	Silica	15
Bentonite	2.9	EPKaolin	33.4	Gerstley borate	5
	100		100		100
Copper carb.	4	Copper carb.	2	Tin oxide	7
				Chromium oxide	3
				Bentonite	2

A12: Bright Chartreuse – cone 06		A12B: Soda Base Glaze (from M. Derby) – cone 04		A12A: Soda Base Glaze (from M. Derby) – cone 04	
Soda ash	70	Soda ash	70	Soda ash	70
EPKaolin	25	EPKaolin	20	EPKaolin	20
Gerstley borate	5	Gerstley borate	10	Gerstley borate	10
	100		100		100
Chromium oxide	5	Chromium oxide	8	Cobalt carb.	3
		Cobalt carb.	3		

A18: Carver Lithium Slip – cone 04		A20 over E16 + SiC – cone 04 A20: Lithium Dry (L. Conway)		A21: Moonellis base glaze (from A. Moran) – cone 04	
		Lithium carb.	14.2	F-4 spar	5
EPKaolin	26	EPKaolin	20.8	Nepheline syenite	55
Zircopax	22	Silica	42.4	Talc	10
Custer spar	22	Frit 3110	11.3	Dolomite	15
Silica	13	Gerstley borate	11.3	Borax	15
Lithium carb.	15		100		100
Bentonite	2	Applied over E16 with 8%		Chromium oxide	3
	100	50-mesh silicon carbide added		Copper carb.	3
Copper carb.	4	to E16.		Bentonite	2

A13B: Bradley's C.B.3 (B. Sabin) – cone 06		A13A: Bradley's C.B.3 (B. Sabin) – cone 06		A17: Todd's 451 Mottled Satin (M. Walsh) – cone 04 (toxic)	
				Kona F4 spar	27.2
Cryolite	46	Cryolite	46	Silica	11
Soda ash	46	Soda ash	46	EPKaolin	13.6
Gerstley borate	8	Gerstley borate	8	Lithium carb.	17.3
	100		100	Barium carb.	14.5
Vanadium pentoxide	5	Manganese dioxide	4	Whiting	5.4
Crimson Mason Stain	5	Cobalt carb.	0.5	Magnesium carb.	11
					100
				Veegum	1

Formulas for alkaline glaze tile set 2

A3: Turquoise Suede (J. Jernegan) – cone 04 (toxic)		A3B: Turquoise Suede (J. Jernegan) – cone 04 (toxic)		A3C: Tan Suede (J. Jernegan) – cone 04 (toxic)	
Lithium carb.	28.1	Lithium carb.	28.1	Lithium carb.	28.1
EPKaolin	10.4	EPKaolin	10.4	EPKaolin	10.4
Calcined kaolin	20.8	Calcined kaolin	20.8	Calcined kaolin	20.8
Bentonite	5.2	Bentonite	5.2	Bentonite	5.2
Silica	35.5	Silica	35.5	Silica	35.5
	100		100		100
Copper carb.	4	Copper carb.	7	Rutile	3
				Red iron oxide	1

A23: Green Moss (F) F. Sundstrom) – cone 04 (toxic)		A5: Chartreuse (from K. Doherty) – cone 04 (toxic)		A20A: Lithium Dry (from L. Conway) – cone 04	
Lithium carb.	80	Lithium carb.	80	Lithium carb.	14.2
Silica	7.5	Gerstley borate	5	EPKaolin	20.8
EPKaolin	7.5	Silica	15	Silica	42.5
Gerstley borate	5		100	Frit 3110	11.3
	100	Bentonite	2	Gerstley borate	11.3
Tin oxide	7	Chromium oxide	3		100
Chromium oxide	3	Tin oxide	7	Copper carb.	2
Bentonite	2				

A20: Lithium Dry (from L. Conway) – cone 04		A25: Craters (B. Shay) – cone 06 (toxic)		A6: Antique Green – cone 10R	
		Lithium carb.	31.6	Nepheline syenite	44
		Silica	31.6	Whiting	15
Lithium carb.	14.2	Borax	15.8	Talc	13
EPKaolin	20.8	Magnesium carb.	10.5	EPKaolin	10
Silica	42.4	EPKaolin	10.5	Zinc oxide	3
Frit 3110	11.3		100	Silica	15
Gerstley borate	11.3				100
	100	Copper carb.	12	Copper carb.	3
		Rutile	10	Rutile	10

A14C: VC Matt variant (from A. Paul) – cone 6		A14B: VC Matt (from A. Paul) – cone 6		A14A: VC Matt (from A. Paul) –cone 6	
Nepheline syenite	40				
Gerstley borate	10	Nepheline syenite	40	Nepheline syenite	40
Lithium carb.	8	Gerstley borate	10	Gerstley borate	10
Whiting	8	Lithium carb.	8	Lithium carb.	8
EPKaolin	10	Whiting	8	Whiting	8
Silica	14	EPKaolin	10	EPKaolin	10
Titanium dioxide	10	Silica	14	Silica	14
	100	Titanium dioxide	10	Titanium dioxide	10
Copper carb.	4		100		100
Cobalt carb.	0.5	Copper carb.	3	Rutile	5
Titanium dioxide	6			Red iron oxide	2

Alkaline glaze tile set 2 (*see formulas opposite*)

White Tongues Red Earth, John Chalke, 2008. Low-alumina, high-white lead glaze with chrome and barium (very similar to BL14, p.76). Fired to cone 04. 39.5cm (15½in.) across. *Photo by Barbara Tipton.*

Chapter 6
Boron, lead and zinc matts

Lead and boron share a unique characteristic. Though quite different chemically, each of them will melt into a pseudo-glass without any other ingredients in the glaze. The surfaces produced are transparent and glossy and relatively soft. They look like conventional silica-based glazes, but may contain no silica at all. Each one has a variety of desirable qualities including predictable, smooth melting, relatively good fit on many clay bodies, and good colour response with many metallic oxides. For this reason each is found in a broad range of mostly low-temperature glazes, both glossy and matt. Lead and boron are both powerful fluxing agents and when used together produce glazes with the lowest melting temperatures, which are used in overglaze enamels and speciality coatings for the electronics industry.

Boric oxide

Due to concerns with toxicity, boron-based glazes have become an important alternative to lead. Of the two, boron is by far the most commonly employed in matt glazes.

Chemically, boric oxide has a form curiously similar to alumina, though its behaviour is very different. Boric oxide acts as a glass former in a glaze as well as a flux. The molecular formula of alumina oxide is Al_2O_3, and of boric oxide is B_2O_3. Both exhibit the same structure, characterised as a neutral refractory oxide, as opposed to a base (a fluxing oxide like sodium (Na_2O)), or an acid (a glass-forming oxide like silica (SiO_2)). While alumina is important in

Primate, Mikey Walsh, 2006. Glazed with BL22 (p.74) on greenware. After bisque firing it was coated with E20 (p.54) red terra sigillata and fired again to cone 04. 51 × 25.5 × 13cm (20 × 10 × 5in.). *Photo by Kevin Duffy.*

Iron V, Lynn Duryea, 2007. Lichen over black slip, sandy molten (BL26, p.74) over lichen and by itself. 62 × 28 × 12.5cm (24½ × 11 × 5in.). *Photo by Troy Tuttle.*

stiffening the glass, and in increasing quantities in moving it to a drier state, boron is a powerful flux that induces melting at very low temperatures. Much has been written about how it should be classified within the Seger/Unity Formula, but for our purposes it is simply a versatile and widely used flux.

The actual melting point of boric oxide is 700°C (1292°F). At low temperatures it produces glossy glazes with good viscosity, but at high temperatures it becomes very fluid, contributing to runny, streaky effects. It is a powerful and useful flux over a wide range of temperatures, though more commonly employed at low temperatures, particularly in dry glazes. Glazes used in the raku process in particular tend to make use of boron as a primary flux (see Chapter 10). Boric oxide shares many of its good qualities as an active low-temperature melting agent with lead oxide, without the major problem of the high toxicity of lead. Boron is soluble in several of its common forms, but has relatively low toxicity. Boron-based matt glazes fall primarily into two of the dry-glaze categories listed: partially melted and sintered matts. Boric oxide has the tendency to inhibit the growth of crystals in a glaze, making it less likely to be found in a devitrified matt glaze. In glazes it gives a low coefficient of expansion.

Colour response

Boric oxide promotes fairly strong colour development, similar to alkaline-based glazes but less vivid. One can expect deep blues from cobalt (see tile BL7, p.76), green-blues from copper (BL15A, p.74), and warm iron reds in matt glazes (BL17A & BL25, p.74) shifting to milky blues from small amounts of iron in more fluid glazes.

Common sources

Borax ($Na_2O_2B_2O_3 10H_2O$)

This is a naturally occurring compound rich in boric oxide and also supplying sodium. It is a highly soluble material, which can make it a bit unpredictable in the glaze. Borax is a powerful flux, with sodium and boron both influencing the melting action. It has a granular form that can be difficult to screen in a glaze. The granules, however, can be important in giving dry glazes a spotted and varied surface, so it is often better to blend the glaze with a whisk or hand-blender than to screen it.

Gerstley borate (or colemanite) ($2CaO_3B_2O_3 5H_2O$)

This is a naturally occurring mineral compound that provides boric oxide and calcium. Colemanite is very similar to gerstley borate, but it should be noted that while they are usually interchangeable, they are not identical. It is the only insoluble source of boric oxide outside of conventional glaze frits. Gerstley borate is an active flux that has been very popular for raku and other earthenware glazes, in part because it has wide firing latitude and is non-toxic. A popular clear-glaze formula for cone 06–1 is 60% gerstley borate and 40% potash feldspar. Reversing the proportions to 40:60 produces a glaze that works from cone 1–6. Gerstley borate goes through an active melting process, boiling and foaming up before melting completely. If the firing is halted before the melt concludes, it results in a lava-type glaze that is foamy and cratered but fragile (see SE16, p.120, Black Lava Glaze). The mineral is a hydrate, meaning that gerstley borate absorbs water in the glaze slop, causing a thickening or gelling of the slop. This characteristic can be helpful in suspending other ingredients but may be a problem in glazes with

Untitled, David Kuraoka, 2007. White slip on stoneware, cone 1 bisque, commercial underglazes and a thin coat of CO18 (p.132), fired to cone 06. 124 x 25 x 18cm (49 x 10 x 7in.). *Photo by Brian Mahany.*

high percentages. Gerstley borate has been mined only in very limited quantities, and is no longer mined. The remaining stocks may last another decade, but synthetic blends exist that have been deliberately produced to closely resemble its formula and behaviour. Laguna Borate, Gillespie Borate and Cadycal are a few of these.

Borax frits

Frits allow the use of boric oxide in an insoluble form, combined with other melting oxides, silica and often alumina. Frits typically melt smoothly, eliminating the foaming and blistering that may be associated with raw sources of boric oxide. Common boron-rich frits include 3124, 3134, 3195, 3454, 2263 and their equivalents from other manufacturers.

Toxicity and health concerns

Low risk: Boron is not considered a toxic element. Gerstley borate is a fairly inert mineral with little hazard. Borax frits have a modest silica-dust inhalation hazard. Borax itself is a strong alkaline compound, is caustic and can cause irritation to the eyes and skin.

Lead oxide

Historically, lead oxide has been extremely important as a glaze ingredient for a variety of reasons. By itself it melts readily and forms a pseudo-glass at very low temperature, approximately 880°C (1660°F). Powdered lead ore (galena) was used by medieval potters to dust onto their still-wet pots to produce a yellow-green glassy coating when fired. Lead melts predictably and smoothly and has a low surface tension, reliably producing a blemish-free surface. It may be used at

Red Can Bay, Jeremy Jernegan, 1994. Ceramic and steel. Various glazes including B5A (p.102) with varied colourants, BL5A and BL14 (p.74 and p.76). In some sections copper wash was used to stain the body and the glaze surface after the first glaze firing in a series of multiple firings. 201 × 30 × 30cm (79 × 12 × 12in.). *Photo by the artist.*

very low temperatures and as high as cone 6, though it does volatilise and should not used above cone 6. It has a high index of refraction and tends to resist recrystallisation upon cooling, making it good for brilliant, clear transparent glaze, though less useful for crystalline matts. Finally, and most importantly for our purposes, it strongly influences colour responses, promoting some brilliant colours, especially in the red and yellow range.

By itself lead produces clear glossy glazes, so matts require a combination of other, more refractory oxides, and/or some degree of under-firing. Thus partially melted and sintered matts are the most common lead-based matt glazes.

Colour response

The primary reason to use lead in a matt glaze is for the colour responses it promotes. Perhaps the best-known and most widely used example is Otto's Texture (BL14, p.76), a vivid orange matt that breaks to green where thin. This dramatic glaze contains chromium oxide, which results commonly in greens, but in the presence of lead (and barium) will produce orange and red hues. Chromium and lead in smaller percentages will also produce yellow and yellow-greens (tile BL12, p.76). Lead in the presence of antimony oxide produces a bright yellow known as Naples Yellow.

Common Sources

Raw lead: red lead (Pb₃O₄) and white lead (2PbCO₃ Pb(OH)₂)

Both of these forms of raw lead are insoluble in water but highly toxic. White lead carbonate is the purer form, with a smaller particle size, and is traditionally preferred by ceramicists.

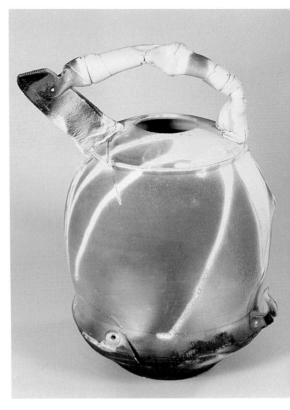

Basket Form, Bryan Vansell, 1982. Glazed with BL13 (p.76) and raku-fired with light post-firing reduction. 56 × 25 × 28cm (22 × 10 × 11in.). *Photo by Doug DeFor.*

Red lead is less pure and has a larger particle size, making it more difficult to suspend in glaze slop. Its bright-orange colour is easily identifiable and thus serves as a constant reminder of the potential health hazard.

Lead frits

Lead bisilicate was one of the earliest forms of fritted lead (which made the use of lead significantly less hazardous) and is still useful as a blend of silica and lead oxide. Fritting binds the lead molecules to silica and makes lead much less dangerous to handle, though it does not eliminate toxicity, particularly if the frit is ingested. Useful lead frits include 3304, 3403, 3485, 3493 and their equivalents.

Toxicity and health concerns

High risk: Lead oxide in its various forms is a dangerous, highly toxic material that may be absorbed by handling through broken skin, inhaled by breathing dust or by breathing vapours during firing, and ingested when soluble glazes come into contact with food. Fritted lead is significantly less toxic than raw lead but is still subject to acid attack. When the human body absorbs lead, it is stored in the tissues and not excreted. This characteristic creates a significant problem if lead is accumulated over a long period of time. Even if the lead intake is small, prolonged exposure over a number of years can result in toxic levels accruing in the body. Lead glazes

should never be considered food-safe without professional testing.

Zinc oxide

Zinc is a metallic oxide and in that way is similar to lead, though not as powerful or toxic. It has a melting point of 1970°C (3578°F), though it begins melting much sooner within many glaze formulas. Historically, it has been important in developing low-lead and lead-free glazes such as the Bristol glaze.[11] It is considered a moderate flux, though is said to be as active as lead in small amounts, and quite refractory in large quantities.[12] Zinc is more common at mid- and high-temperature ranges as a flux. At earthenware temperatures it is generally refractory. Increasing quantities of zinc in a glaze will influence it to become opaque and ultimately quite matt. It can be added to a glaze specifically to make it an opaque and devitrified

Marking Time, Jeremy Jernegan, 1994. Various glazes including BL5A (p.74) and A3 (p.64). Copper wash was used to stain the body and the glaze surface after the first glaze firing in a series of multiple firings to cone 06–04. 114 × 305 × 30cm (45 × 120 × 12in.). *Photo by the artist.*

matt (see pp.12, 13 and 17). Zinc oxide promotes the growth of crystals in the cooling glaze matrix, particularly in low-alumina glazes, and it is used as a primary flux in some macrocrystalline glazes. It is occasionally used in very large amounts (60%) to produce special-effect-type 'shrink and crawl' glazes. These are typically sintered matts that pull apart during the firing due to the high shrinkage rate of raw zinc oxide (see Chapter 9). Zinc oxide has a moderately low coefficient of expansion, similar to calcium and barium oxides.

Colour response

Zinc has a fairly dramatic effect on colour, though not necessarily in a positive way. Zinc can interfere with the colour development of a number of common ceramic stains, particularly the chrome-tin pink and maroon hues. Zinc tends to produce murky colours with raw oxides, particularly with chrome and iron. Colour response from cobalt oxide can range from strong blue to dark green in high-zinc glazes (see tile SE7, p.116).

Common sources

Zinc oxide (ZnO)

This is the most common source and is available in both raw and calcined form. Calcined zinc is chemically the same but does not shrink during the firing, avoiding problems with crawling (a good thing when crawling is not wanted). Crawl glazes must use raw zinc oxide to work. It is insoluble in water in both forms.

Zinc zirconium silicate ($ZnOZrO_2SiO_2$)

This is a commercially prepared frit combining zinc, zirconium and silica. It is most commonly introduced into glazes as an opacifier and is insoluble in water.

Toxicity and health concerns

Low to medium risk: Zinc oxide is not considered a hazardous substance.[13] However, during glaze firings it volatises at low temperatures in a reduction atmosphere, creating a hazard from fumes exiting the kiln. Glazes with high concentrations of zinc may release zinc into solutions, creating a potential ingestion hazard.

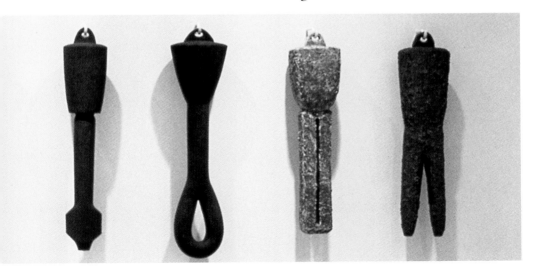

Formulas for boron and lead glaze tile set 1

BL15: Jacquie's Base (from M. Bohls) – cone 06	
Gerstley borate	33.9
Lithium carb.	8.9
Nepheline syenite	4.5
EPKaolin	4.5
Whiting	10.7
Silica	37.5
	100
Tin oxide	5
Blue mason stain 6363	10

BL15C: Jacquie's Base (from M. Bohls) – cone 06	
Gerstley borate	33.9
Lithium carb.	8.9
Nepheline syenite	4.5
EPKaolin	4.5
Whiting	10.7
Silica	37.5
	100
Tin oxide	5

BL15B: Jacquie's Base (from M. Bohls) – cone 06	
Gerstley borate	33.9
Lithium carb.	8.9
Nepheline syenite	4.5
EPKaolin	4.5
Whiting	10.7
Silica	37.5
	100
Copper carb.	4

BL18: Stony Quartz (from P. Pemberton) – cone 04	
Gerstley borate	38
Lithium carb.	10
Nepheline syenite	5
EPKaolin	5
Silica	42
	100
Ultrox	5

BL15A: Jacquie's Base (from M. Bohls) – cone 06	
Gerstley borate	30
Spodumene	20
Silica	50
	100
Copper carb.	3

BL2: Crusty Matt – cone 05	
EPKaolin	40
Borax	40
Silica	20
	100
Copper carb.	4
Cobalt carb.	4

BL22: Tar Black (from M. Walsh) – cone 04 (toxic)	
Gerstley borate	50
Borax	39
Silica	11
	100
Iron chromate	17
Rutile	11
Cobalt oxide	11
Copper oxide	11

BL25: Velvet Crust (from L. Duryea) – cone 04	
Gerstley borate	42.4
Nepheline syenite	14.2
Alumina hydrate	43.4
	100
Red iron oxide	4

BL26: Sandy Molten (from L. Duryea) – cone 04	
Borax	30
Redart clay	30
Silica	40
	100

BL5B: Dry Base – cone 06	
Gerstley borate	50
Alumina hydrate	33.3
Nepheline syenite	16.7
	100
Pansy purple Mason stain No. 6385	15

BL5A: Dry Base – cone 06	
Gerstley borate	50
Alumina hydrate	33.3
Nepheline syenite	16.7
	100
Yellow Mason stain No. 6450	20

BL5D: Dry Base – cone 06	
Gerstley borate	50
Alumina hydrate	33.3
Nepheline syenite	16.7
	100
Degussa orange stain	15

Boron and lead glaze tile set 1 (*see formulas opposite*)

BL14: Otto's Texture (O. Heino) – cone 06 (toxic)		BL13: Dry Yellow (B. Vansell) – cone 06 (toxic)		BL12: Lead Yellow – cone 06 (toxic)	
Red lead	62.1	Gerstley borate	25	Lead bisilicate	69.4
Custer spar	20	Red lead	30	Barium carb.	17.3
EPKaolin	4.2	Borax	12.5	EPKaolin	13.3
Barium carb.	9.5	Soda ash	12.5		100
Cornwall stone	4.2	Antimony oxide	12.5		
	100	Tin oxide	7.5	Chromium oxide	2.5
			100		
Chromium oxide	4				
Bentonite	2				

BL8: Deadly Chartreuse – cone 04 (toxic)		BL17A: Bates (from V. Burke) – cone 04		BL17C: Bates (from V. Burke) – cone 04	
Lead bisilicate	80	Borax	25	Borax	25
Barium carb.	20	Spodumene	25	Spodumene	25
	100	EPKaolin	50	EPKaolin	50
			100		100
Chromium oxide	2.5				
Bentonite	3	Red iron oxide	4	Cobalt carb.	0.5
				Copper carb.	2

BL21: Rutile Borax Matt (K. Martz) – cone 04		BL3: Dry Lavender Glaze – cone 05		BL4: Watershed Stone – cone 04	
				EPKaolin	21.7
Potash spar	11	Plastic vitrox	30	Ball clay	21.7
Whiting	16	Gerstley borate	30	Gerstley borate	21.7
Ball clay	10	Silica	40	Silica	21.7
Borax	42		100	Lithium carb.	13.2
Rutile	21				100
	100	Cobalt carb.	4		
				Rutile	4
				Granular ilmenite (add after screening)	5

BL23: Alligator – cone 04		BL1: Ultra Dry White – cone 06		BL7: Green Velvet Crust – cone 04	
Gerstley borate	57.1			Gerstley borate	49
Nepheline syenite	14.3	Plastic vitrox	30	Nepheline syenite	16
Bone ash	28.6	Silica	40	Alumina hydrate	35
	100	Gerstley borate	30		100
			100		
Copper carb.	3			Cobalt carb.	2
				Rutile	1

Covered Jar Column Series, Val Cushing, 2002. Glazed with mix of 60% MC36 and 40% MC37 (p.88), with added oxide wash on the bottom section. The top section is MC35 (see also p.88). Fired to cone 91.5cm (36in.) tall. *Photo by Seth Tice Lewis.*

Chapter 7

Calcium and magnesium matts

Calcium and magnesium are indispensable in formulating what are often considered the classic matt glazes. These include a range of microcrystalline matts that are completely melted, smooth and suitable for a variety of surfaces, from sculpture to utilitarian tableware. These devitrified matts are typically high-temperature glazes in muted hues that may show the characteristic iron spotting of reduction-fired stoneware. Such glazes are smooth and soft to the touch, ranging from buttery to eggshell to stony surfaces. Calcium and magnesium matts tend to be very durable, with hard, dense surfaces that resist scratching and abrasion. Glazes rich in these oxides are excellent choices for ceramic artists who want to avoid toxic materials and work with food-safe glazes. Both oxides are quite inert and nearly insoluble in most common forms, making them quite safe and easy to work with. So popular and widely used, calcium and magnesium matt glazes are what many people think of when one mentions a matt glaze.

Calcium oxide

Calcium is used as a flux but has a very high melting point 2570°C (4658°F). Like the other alkaline earth metals (magnesium, strontium and barium) it is usually dissolved into the melt with the aid of other fluxes in the glaze. Curiously, calcium is generally considered a flux of low activity, but at high temperatures it becomes very active and promotes significant melting. It is one of the most widely used glaze fluxes at temperatures above cone 010 (890°C/1634°F) and contributes a number of good characteristics to a glaze.[14] Calcium is a predictable and dependable fluxing oxide that does not volatilise and can be used over a wide range of temperatures. Even in modest amounts calcium increases the hardness and durability of a glaze, allowing it to resist weathering and acid attack. Calcium oxide is widely available, inexpensive and non-toxic in most forms. Glazes with moderate to large amounts of calcium tend to devitrify during the cooling cycle and form microcrystalline structures, resulting in the opaque matts so characteristic of calcium. The crystals formed in such matts are made up of anothite, a calcium feldspar.[15] In large quantities and at lower temperatures, calcium may act as a refractory oxide, resulting in partially melted matts that may have a very rough and stony surface. Calcium has a moderate to low coefficient of expansion, on a par with barium and strontium.

Colour response

Calcium is relatively neutral in its influence on colour, and not associated with particularly bright or intense hues. It is said to have a slight bleaching effect on iron, favouring pale celadon grey-greens (see tile MC28C, p.92). 'High-lime' matts may be yellowish with the addition of iron, instead of orange or

Creation Form, Jim Robinson, 1995. Glazed with MC34 (p.84). Fired to cone 10. 25 × 61cm (10 × 24in.). *Photo by Robert Jaffe.*

brown (See tile MC37, p.88).[16] Calcium is helpful in developing copper reds and purples in reduction.

Common sources

Whiting or calcium carbonate ($CaCO_3$)

This a major source of relatively pure calcium oxide, produced from ground chalk, marble or limestone. Parmalee observes that the low specific gravity of the carbonate helps it remain suspended in glaze slop and assists the suspension of other heavier ingredients.[17] Whiting can cause blistering or bubbling in glazes due to the large amount of carbon-dioxide gas liberated during the firing. It is insoluble in water.

Wollastonite ($CaOSiO_2$)

This is a naturally occurring calcium silicate providing a good source for both calcium and silica. Wollastonite is perhaps the best way to introduce calcium and silica in conventional glazes due to its smooth and uniform melting characteristics and limited shrinkage. It is also favoured for clay-body additions as a low-activity flux and for its needle-like crystalline structure, which is an asset in green strength and reducing thermal shock. It is insoluble in water.

Dolomite ($CaCo_3MgCO_3$)

This is a good source of calcium and magnesium oxides in equal proportions. Many high-temperature matts make use of dolomite as an inexpensive, insoluble and convenient way to introduce these complementary oxides. Liberation of carbon dioxide during the firing can again cause bubbling or blistering in a glaze without sufficient time to heal over prior to cooling.

Bone ash ($Ca_3(PO_4)_2$)

This provides calcium phosphate from calcined animal bones. It contributes calcium to a glaze and also phosphorous, which may result in bubbling and boiling of the glaze surface. These bubbles also contribute opacity and opalescence to a glaze. Bone ash is used in large quantities in some very dry earthenware and mid-range glazes to develop a sandy textural surface in sintered and partially melted matts. It is slightly soluble in water. Tri-calcium phosphate (TCP) is sometimes called for as a synthetic equivalent of bone ash.

Cornwall stone feldspar

This is a modest source of calcium combined with roughly equal parts of sodium and potassium oxides, as well as silica and alumina. Many types of feldspar contain very small amounts of calcium, but Cornwall stone is the only significant source. It is insoluble in water.

Gerstley borate or colemanite ($2CaO_3B_2O_3 5H_2O$)

This is a very useful source of calcium and boric oxide in a naturally occurring frit-like compound. It is a powerful flux and is commonly used in earthenware glazes and in a limited way in high-fire glazes (see Chapters 6 & 10). It is somewhat soluble in water, but expands when wetted and will cause the glaze slop to gel. Note that although gerstley borate and colemanite are usually interchangeable, they are not identical.

Various calcium-rich glaze frits
In part because of their cost, frits are not a common way to introduce calcium as a primary flux. Ferro frits 3124, 4112 and 3271, and Fusion frits F2 and F13, contain calcium oxide, silica and various additional oxides. Most frits are insoluble in water.

Magnesium oxide

Magnesium has the highest melting point of all the common fluxing oxides, 2800°C (5072°F), but it forms eutectics (see p.141) with other materials and functions as an effective flux at high temperatures. Like calcium it is most effective at stoneware temperatures and tends to act as a refractory oxide at low temperatures, particularly in large quantities.

In such cases magnesium forms partially melted matts in which the largely unmelted magnesium oxide remains suspended as a refractory opacifier. While not widely used in glazes at low temperatures, it is common as an earthenware body flux in the form of talc, a magnesium silicate. In that form it appears to develop a eutectic with the constituents of the clay and encourages gradual fusion from the earthenware temperature range to mid-range temperatures.

ABOVE *Let's Go Teapot #15*, Barbara Frey, 2001. Glazed with MC50 (p.86) and coloured porcelain slip and inlay. Fired to cone 6. 18.5 × 16.5 × 16.5cm (7¼ × 6½ × 6½in.). *Photo by Harrison Evans.*

RIGHT *Cerberus*, Susan Bowers, 2008. White slip on stoneware, glazed with MC42 (p.88). Fired to cone 10R. 43 × 41 × 28cm (17 × 16 × 11in.). *Photo by the author.*

Orange Tea Bowl, John Oles, 2008. Porcelain glazed with MC33 sprayed over MC32 (p.92). Fired to cone 9. 10 × 11.5cm (4 × 4½in.). *Photo by the artist.*

Perhaps the most important behaviour of magnesium is that at high temperatures it influences a glaze to devitrify upon cooling and to grow an opaque microcrystalline structure. The crystals that form within the cooled glaze are composed of enstatite, a pure magnesium silicate.[18] Typically too tiny to see with the naked eye, the crystalline structure results in the unique eggshell-type matt surfaces that magnesium is known for. These matts are typically smooth and soft to the touch, and may show the evidence of fluidity without any apparent gloss.

Magnesium and calcium are often introduced together in the form of dolomite, with each complementing the characteristics of the other. Dolomite matts, as they are sometimes known, tend to be durable and stable, and are widely used on all types of ware. Magnesium has a very low coefficient of expansion, in fact the lowest of any common fluxing oxide. While glazes rich in calcium or magnesium are not likely to have crazing problems, high-magnesium glazes may have so little contraction on cooling that shivering could result on some clay bodies.

Colour response

Neither calcium oxide nor magnesium oxide encourages strong or saturated colours. On the contrary, they both tend toward muted and low-saturation colour, particularly in high concentrations. Magnesium oxide has a more distinctive impact on colour in that it will influence the development of pastel hues. Used with cobalt it tends to result in unique lavender and purple shades (see tiles MC3, MC7B, p.86) and with copper produces murky grey-pinks, and can blush pink from the fuming of nearby copper glazes.

Common sources

Dolomite (CaCo₃MgCO₃)

As noted in the previous section, this is a good and inexpensive source of calcium and magnesium oxides in equal proportions.

Magnesium carbonate (MgCO₃)

This is the pure form of magnesium and a popular source for adding small quantities to a glaze. It has a fluffy character and a very low density, which causes it to absorb large amounts of water in the glaze slop and can result in significant shrinkage during the firing. The pronounced shrinkage often leads to glaze crawling, normally a serious flaw. However, magnesium carbonate is intentionally used in large quantities in special 'shrink and crawl' glazes to exploit this characteristic (see Chapter 9). It is slightly water-soluble.

Talc (3MgO 4SiO₂ H₂O)

Talc ($3MgO \cdot 4SiO_2 \cdot H_2O$)

This is a naturally occurring magnesium silicate, inexpensive and insoluble in water. Talc is also a common body flux for white earthenware clays.

Toxicity and health concerns

Low risk: Neither calcium nor magnesium are considered toxic elements. They are relatively inert and non-reactive in most forms, with little to no solubility. Glazes compounded with them are among the most stable and non-reactive. The primary concern with these materials is the chronic inhalation hazard of dusts containing silica and silica-like substances. Talc may contain small amounts of impurities, including asbestos, and thus particular care should be taken to avoid breathing the dust.

Storage Jar, Acorn Series, Val Cushing, 2001. Glazed with MC39 (p.88) and B15 base 3% RIO (p.102) on rim. Fired to cone 10. Ht: 36cm (14in.). *Photo by Seth Tice Lewis.*

Cut Rim Bowl, Greg Daly, 2005. Glazed with MC44 (p.92) and fired in oxidation to cone 8. Dia: 34cm (13¹/₂in.). *Photo by Stuart Hay.*

Formulas for calcium and magnesium glaze (MC) tile set 1

MC19: Matt Yellow (P. Horsley) – cone 6

Unispar	11.9
Whiting	23.8
EPKaolin	47.6
Wood ash	16.7
	100
Frit 3124	4
Ochre	5

MC20: 1879 Rust Red (P. Horsley) – cone 10R

Custer spar	17.8
Whiting	28.6
EPKaolin	53.6
	100
Frit 3124	10
Tri-calcium phosphate	4
Red iron oxide	4

MC9: Crusty Calcium – cone 10R

Whiting	30
Bone ash	50
EPKaolin	20
	100
Red iron oxide	1

MC12: Cindy Yellow – cone 10R

Potash spar	34.9
Whiting	3.5
Dolomite	19.2
EPKaolin	21.8
Rutile	20.6
	100

MC22: Silica Crust A – cone 10R

Cornwall stone	28
Whiting	12
EPKaolin	17
Silica	43
	100
Red iron oxide	2

MC18: Grey/Pink/Blue Matt – cone 6

Barium carb.	10.4
Lithium carb.	2.6
Whiting	23.4
Nepheline syenite	51.9
Kaolin	11.7
	100
Chromium oxide	0.5
Cobalt carb.	0.25
Manganese dioxide	0.5
Tin oxide	8

MC1: Pale Dolomitic Matt – cone 10R

Custer spar	35
EPKaolin	12
Ball clay	17
Whiting	12
Silica	7
Dolomite	17
	100

MC2: Binns Rutile – cone 10R

Whiting	24
Custer spar	61
EPKaolin	15
	100
Rutile	5

MC2B: Binns Rutile Variant – cone 10R

Whiting	24
Custer spar	61
EPKaolin	15
	100
Rutile	10

MC34: R1928 (J. Robinson) – cone 10R

Molochite	55
EPKaolin	10
G22 spar	5
Whiting	20
Bone ash	10
	100
Copper carb.	3
Veegum	0.5

MC43C: High Alumina Dry Matt (G. Daly) – cone 10R

Potash spar	20
Whiting	10
Silica	15
Kaolin	5
Alumina hydrate	50
	100
Red iron oxide	2
Titanium dioxide	5

MC43B: High Alumina Dry Matt (G. Daly) – cone 10R

Potash spar	20
Whiting	10
Silica	15
Kaolin	5
Alumina hydrate	50
	100
Cobalt carb.	4

Calcium and magnesium glaze (MC) tile set 1 (*see formulas opposite*)

Formulas for calcium and magnesium glaze (MC) tile set 2

MC17: Frosty Clear (J. Jernegan) – cone 10R

Calcined kaolin	24
EPKaolin	9
Whiting	31.5
Potash spar	16
Silica	15
Nepheline syenite	4.5
	100

MC16B: Jenny's Dolomite (J. Long) – cone 10R

Custer spar	49
EPKaolin	25
Dolomite	22
Whiting	4
	100
Red iron oxide	3
Rutile	4
Tin oxide	3

MC3: LP Matt (V. Cushing) – cone 10R

Potash spar	30
Dolomite	20
EPKaolin	15
Calcined kaolin	10
Barium carb.	15
Silica	10
	100
Cobalt carb.	1
Manganese dioxide	0.5

MC30D: Pebble Metallic (G. Daly) – cone 10R

Nepheline syenite	12
Whiting	10.4
Silica	12
EPKaolin	5.6
Bone ash	60
	100
Red iron oxide	10

MC6: Black Matt – cone 10R

Potash spar	37
Cornwall stone	19
Whiting	19
EPKaolin	9
Calcined zinc oxide	6
Calcined kaolin	10
	100
Red iron oxide	12
Manganese dioxide	1
Cobalt carb.	2

MC7B: Semi-dry Lavender – cone 10R

EPKaolin	10
Silica	10
Spodumene	30
Talc	50
	100
Cobalt carb.	2

MC26: Peter Holtzen Mottled Purple – cone 6

Petalite	40
EPKaolin	17
Dolomite	17
Whiting	6
Silica	10
Cobalt oxide	10
	100

MC26A: Peter Holtzen Mottled Purple Variant – cone 6

Petalite	40
EPKaolin	17
Dolomite	17
Whiting	6
Silica	10
Cobalt oxide	10
	100
Titanium dioxide	10

MC51: White Matt (B. Frey) – cone 6

Minspar	61.9
Dolomite	20.6
Barium carb.	15.5
Bentonite	2
	100
Zircopax	8

MC19B: Ying Ching (from G. Gibson) – cone 6

Frit 3110	20
Zinc oxide	20
Whiting	20
Silica	36
Bentonite	4
	100
Copper carb.	2

MC19A: Ying Ching (from G. Gibson) – cone 6

Frit 3110	20
Zinc oxide	20
Whiting	20
Silica	36
Bentonite	4
	100
Rutile	10

MC50: Turquoise Matt (B. Frey) – cone 6

Minspar	61.9
Dolomite	20.6
Barium carb.	15.5
Bentonite	2
	100
Copper carb.	2

Calcium and magnesium glaze (MC) tile set 2 (*see formulas opposite*)

Formulas for calcium and magnesium glaze (MC) tile set 3

MC36: Mamo Matt (V. Cushing) – cone 10R		MC38: Spodumene (V. Cushing) – cone 10R		MC41: Lanman Fake Ash (V. Cushing) – cone 10R	
Kona F-4 Spar	50	Custer spar	30	Custer spar	15
Dolomite	20	Spodumene	20	Whiting	30
Whiting	4	Dolomite	22	Dolomite	9
EPKaolin	10	Whiting	4	Barium carb.	9
Calcined EPK	11	EPKaolin	24	Ball clay	18
Tin oxide	5		100	Silica	19
	100				100
		Tin oxide	5		
				Red iron oxide	6

MC42: Apple Ash (V. Cushing) – cone 10R		MC35: AA Revised (V. Cushing) – cone 10R		MC39A: AA Taffy Matt (V. Cushing) – cone 10R	
Apple wood ash	60	Cornwall stone	51.2	Cornwall stone	46
Cornwall stone	10	Whiting	35.6	Whiting	34
EPKaolin	24	Dolomite	4.4	EPKaolin	20
Titanium dioxide	6	Titanium dioxide	4.4		100
	100	EPKaolin	4.4		
			100	Copper carb.	4
				Tin oxide	4
		Tin oxide	2		
		Cobalt carb.	0.15		

MC39: AA Taffy Matt (V. Cushing) – cone 10R		MC4: Stony Matt (from J. Zeller) – cone 10R		MC40: Tomato Red (V. Cushing) – cone 10R	
				Kona F-4 spar	45
Cornwall stone	46	Nepheline syenite	16.9	Whiting	7
Whiting	34	Whiting	3.6	Bone ash	11
EPKaolin	20	Dolomite	13.6	Silica	24
	100	Talc	13.6	Grolleg kaolin	7
Red iron oxide	4	EPKaolin	25.3	Magnesium carb.	6
Titanium dioxide	6	Cornwall stone	25.5		100
		Gerstley borate	1.5		
			100	Red iron oxide	8
				Bentonite	2

MC8: Rich Matt – cone 10R		MC37: Shaner Red Matte (V. Cushing) – cone 10R		MC20B: Nick's Misfire (from M. Bohls) – cone 10R	
Custer spar	50			Nepheline syenite	42.2
Dolomite	20	Custer spar	52	Whiting	15.8
EPKaolin	20	Whiting	21	Talc	10.5
Bone ash	10	Talc	4	EPKaolin	10.5
	100	Calcined EPKaolin	8	Silica	10.5
		EPKaolin	15	Tin oxide	10.5
Vanadium pentoxide	5		100		100
Powdered illmenite	3				
Chromium oxide	1	Red iron oxide	4	Cobalt carb.	0.25
Tin oxide	2.5	Bone ash	4	Rutile	2.0

Formulas for calcium and magnesium glaze (MC) tile set 4

MC5: Dolomite Matt – cone 10R

Potash spar	49
EPKaolin	25
Dolomite	22
Whiting	4
	100
Cobalt carb.	0.075
Copper carb.	0.15

MC22A2: Talc Matt Glaze – cone 10R

Talc	36
Whiting	11
Nepheline syenite	24
Kaolin	19
Titanium dioxide	10
	100

MC25; VC Satin Doll Black revised (H. Deller) – cone 10R. (toxic)

Redart clay	44.4
Nepheline syenite	16.7
Barium carb.	11.1
Talc	16.7
Whiting	11.1
	100
Chromium oxide	1
Red iron oxide	2
Manganese dioxide	2
Cobalt carb.	2

MC13: C-6 Matt – cone 10R

Potash spar	55
Whiting	25
EPKaolin	10
Calcined kaolin	10
	100
Cobalt carb.	0.25
Nickel carb.	1.25
Rutile	3.5

MC10: Textural Bone Matt – cone 10R

Potash spar	27.5
Dolomite	20.8
EPKaolin	17.2
Bone ash	34.5
	100

MC15B: Silky Matt – cone 10R

Potash spar	28.5
EPKaolin	28
Silica	15
Dolomite	19
Wollastonite	5.5
Gerstley borate	4
	100
Cobalt carb.	3
Vanadium pentoxide	2

MC11: Cream Stone – cone 10R

Nepheline syenite	50
Whiting	5
Dolomite	15
Talc	5
Ball clay	10
EPKaolin	10
Silica	5
	100

MC1: Pale Dolomitic Matt – cone 10R

Custer spar	35
EPKaolin	12
Ball clay	17
Whiting	12
Silica	7
Dolomite	17
	100

MC7C: Very Dry Lavender – cone 10R

EPKaolin	10
Silica	10
Spodumene	20
Talc	60
	100
Cobalt carb.	2

MC21: Mustard – cone 10R

Potash spar	56.3
Whiting	20.7
EPKaolin	17.3
Zinc oxide	5.7
	100
Red iron oxide	5
Rutile	12

MC15A: Silky Matt – cone 10R

Potash spar	28.5
EPKaolin	28
Silica	15
Dolomite	19
Wollastonite	5.5
Gerstley borate	4
	100
Vanadium pentoxide	5

MC14: Opaque Orange Matt – cone 10R

Custer spar	48.2
Whiting	17.7
EPKaolin	14.7
Rutile	8.7
Ultrox	5.4
Red iron oxide	4.3
Bentonite	1.0
	100

Calcium and magnesium glaze (MC) tile set 4 (*see formulas opposite*)

Formulas for calcium and magnesium glaze (MC) tile set 5

MC30A: Gold Matt (G. Daly) – cone 10R		MC30B: Crystal Matt (G. Daly) – cone 10R		MC30C: Limonite Crystal (G. Daly) – cone 10R	
Nepheline syenite	27.2	Nepheline syenite	21	Nepheline syenite	18
Whiting	23.8	Whiting	18.2	Whiting	15.6
Silica	27.2	Silica	21	Silica	18
EPKaolin	12.7	EPKaolin	9.8	EPKaolin	8.4
Titanium dioxide	9.1	Titanium dioxide	30	Titanium dioxide	40
	100		100		100
Red iron oxide	10	Red iron oxide	10	Red iron oxide	10

MC31: Coleman Base – cone 10R		MC32: Dolomite Base (from J. Oles) – cone 10R		MC33: Orange (J. Oles) – cone 10R	
G200 spar	37			Nepheline syenite	40
Whiting	14	Potash spar	50	Whiting	8
Barium carb.	13	Dolomite	20	Silica	14
EPKaolin	11.5	EPKaolin	20	EPKaolin	10
Gerstley borate	6	Bone ash	10	Gerstley borate	10
Lithium carb.	4		100	Lithium carb.	8
Zinc oxide	0.5			Titanium dioxide	10
Titanium dioxide	14	Rutile	11		100
	100				
				Red iron oxide	5

MC28A1: Variegated Tan Matt – cone 10R		MC28B1: Broken Tan – cone 10R		MC28C: Pale Green Matt – cone 10R	
G200 spar	22.4	G200 spar	27.7	G200 spar	70
Whiting	36.6	Whiting	45.3	Whiting	30
EPKaolin	30	EPKaolin	27		100
Silica	11		100		
	100			Red iron oxide	1
Red iron oxide	1	Red iron oxide	1		
Rutile	5	Rutile	5		

MC28A: Variegated Matt – cone 10R		MC28C1 – cone 10R		MC44: (G. Daly) – cone 9R	
		G200 spar	64.8	Nepheline syenite	55
		Whiting	30.6	Whiting	16
G200 spar	22.4	EPKaolin	4.6	Talc	13
Whiting	36.6		100	EPKaolin	16
EPKaolin	30				100
Silica	11	Bentonite	2		
	100	Red iron oxide	1	Copper carb.	4
Red iron oxide	1				

Calcium and magnesium glaze (MC) tile set 5 (*see formulas opposite*)

Large Tea Pot, Patrick Horsley, 2006. Glazed with B4 (p.100). 53 × 53 × 11.5cm (21 × 21 × 4½in.). *Photo by Courtney Frisse.*

Chapter 8

Barium and strontium matts

Barium-based matt glazes are some of the most popular for two important reasons. Firstly, barium influences the development of a crystalline structure in the cooling glaze, resulting in a particularly appealing satin surface which is similar to a magnesium matt but a bit smoother. Second, barium intensifies the colour response of many colouring oxides, producing brilliant and saturated hues that mottle or break dramatically when the glaze goes from thick to thin. The way barium influences glazes to shift colour, depending on the thickness of the glaze, gives it great potential for creating glaze surfaces of

visual complexity and depth. This characteristic is exploited by artists through the application and selective removal of glaze (see Chapter 3).

Moderate amounts of barium (5–10%) will contribute noticeably to colour development in many glazes. High percentages of barium tend to produce very dry matt glazes, even at high temperatures. These surfaces can be brilliantly coloured, particularly with blues from cobalt and turquoise from copper, and tend to break or shift in colour over texture, making them favourites for sculptural pieces. One of the drawbacks with barium is that it is

Be Still…, Kathleen Royster Lamb, 1998. Porcelainous stoneware. Glazed with B3A (p.100), applied and partially wiped off. Fired to cone 10. 16.5 × 30.5 × 16.5cm (6½ × 12 × 6½in.). *Photo by the artist.*

Tinus, Scott Chamberlain, 1993. Glazed with a variant of B23 (p.106). Fired to cone 06. 183 × 183 × 91.5cm (72 × 72 × 36in.). *Photo by John Bonath.*

poisonous in its common raw state of barium carbonate, and barium-rich glazes may leach barium into food and drink if used on tableware. Strontium carbonate, which is non -toxic, is sometimes used as a substitute and shares some of the positive characteristics of barium, but not all.

Barium oxide

Barium oxide (BaO) has a high melting point, 1923°C (3493°F) but is a moderately active flux, commonly used at mid-range and high temperatures. It is usually viewed as more active than the other so-called alkaline earth metals of calcium, magnesium and strontium, but requires a significant amount of heat to initiate the melting process. Richard and Douglas Eppler observe that in each case the melting point is high enough that in normal circumstances the material must be first dissolved into the melted glaze, after which it acts as a flux.[19]

This explains the tendency of high-barium glazes to maintain the characteristics of a sintered matt even at high temperatures. Once it is dissolved, barium can function as quite an active flux, producing fluid glazes. At low temperatures barium acts more as a refractory oxide, matting the glaze surface and producing partially melted or sintered matt glazes. Barium interacts significantly with boric oxide, forming a eutectic that can result in very vigorous melting.

Matt glazes featuring barium range from relatively balanced glazes with modest percentages (10–15%) of barium working in concert with other fluxes, to those with very high percentages (30–70%), which are quite dramatic, unconventional and very dry. In the first type barium can contribute to strong colour response and add to a soft crystalline matt quality. There is evidence that a properly compounded glaze containing up to 15% barium has low-enough solubility to be safe to use on functional ware. However, most ceramicists elect to play it safe and avoid barium glazes for any surfaces that come into contact with food. Barium has a moderate to low coefficient of expansion, similar to calcium and lithium.

Colour response

Barium enhances the colour response of most colouring oxides. It produces vivid turquoise from copper, similar to the alkaline fluxes but even brighter and deeper. Cobalt can produce an intense blue, almost fluorescent in its saturation. Small amounts of barium favour celadon-greens with iron, while larger amounts encourage iron-blues.[20] Variation in the thickness of barium glazes often results in dramatic colour shifts or breaks. For instance, a thick application of a copper-bearing glaze may be deep aquamarine, while thinner areas may be pale turquoise.

Common sources

Barium carbonate (BaCO₃)

Barium carbonate ($BaCO_3$)
This is the pure form of barium, widely used to introduce barium oxide in a glaze. It can produce blistering in the glaze due to the high temperature at which the carbonate breaks down and liberates carbon-dioxide gas into the melted glaze.[21] Barium carbonate is quite toxic and must be handled with care. It is insoluble in water.

Barium-rich frits

These include Fusion F403, Pemco P-626, Ferro 3289, 3247 and 3257. They introduce barium oxide, silica and other

Iron 2X2, Lynn Duryea, 2007. Glazed with combinations of crust glazes (BL25, p.74), and Sandy Molten (BL26, p.74) over Shin Li (SE40, p.116). 39.5 × 30.5 × 12.5cm (15½ × 12 × 5in.). *Photo by Troy Tuttle.*

compounds. Substituting a frit for barium carbonate makes a glaze less dangerous to handle and may make it less soluble when fired. To accurately substitute a frit you must recalculate the glaze formula by hand or with the use of a glaze calculation programme like Insight by Digital Fire. Most frits are insoluble in water.

Strontium oxide

Historically, **strontium oxide (SrO)** was seen as similar to and a potential substitute for calcium oxide and zinc oxide. It acts in a similar way, though it is a bit more fusible. With a high melting point of 2430°C (4406°F), it is only moderately active at high temperatures but has a long

Sea Lion Basket, Jim Robinson, 1991. Glazed with B33 (p.100) fired to cone 10. Ht: 66cm (26in.). *Photo by Robert Jaffe.*

Hon, Scott Chamberlain, 1999. Glazed with B22 (p.106). Fired to cone 06. 46 × 31 × 31cm (18 × 12 × 12in.). *Photo by John Bonath.*

firing range and contributes to crystalline matts in higher quantities.

Frank & Janet Hamer assert that when introduced as a frit strontium oxide may be used at all temperatures, but if introduced as strontium carbonate it is only appropriate at temperatures above 1090°C (1994°F).[22] In high percentages (25+% at cone 04, 60+% at cone 10) strontium has a strong matting effect, particularly at low temperatures. More recently, in studio ceramic practice strontium has become popular as a substitute for barium, eliminating barium's toxicity hazard while

mimicking some of its colour responses (though in truth the colour response is somewhat different, if still bright). Strontium carbonate is non-toxic and is typically substituted for three quarters (or even less) of the weight of barium carbonate called for in a formula, i.e. 0.75 g of strontium for 1 g of barium.[24] One drawback is that strontium is considerably more expensive than either barium or calcium. Strontium has a coefficient of expansion that is almost the same as barium, just slightly less. For this reason both barium- and strontium-rich glazes are less likely to craze on a given clay body, and in regard to their co-efficient of expansion are more or less safely interchangeable.

Colour response

Strontium has a colour response that is similar but not identical to barium. In general the colour is not as saturated and the hues are less pure. Because its melting behaviour and interaction with other materials is not identical, direct comparisons are problematic. However, for comparison glaze tile B24 (p.106) is a particularly intense barium blue coloured with 3% copper carbonate while tile B24A (p.106) is a similar formula substituting strontium, and the result is quite a muted blue-grey.

Common sources

Strontium carbonate (SrCO₃)

This is the only readily available source for raw strontium oxide. It is slightly water-soluble.

Strontium-rich glaze frits

These include Pemco P-4K47, P786, P930, and Fusion F18, F38, F506 and F300. Most frits are insoluble in water.

Toxicity and health concerns

High to low risk: Barium carbonate is highly toxic and considerable care is needed when handling the raw material and the unfired glaze. Any glaze containing more than 20% barium should not be used on surfaces that come into contact with food, and those with less than 20% should still be tested for solubility before use on these same surfaces. Strontium is not considered toxic and may be used as a safer alternative to barium. As with any powdered material, care should be taken to avoid inhaling the dust.

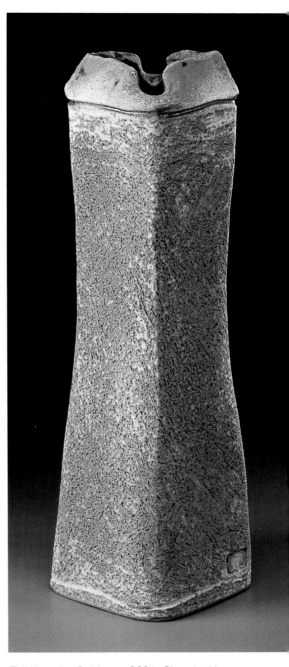

Tall Vase, Jim Robinson, 2004. Glazed with B33 (p.100) sprayed over a wash of an Alberta slip glaze. Fired to cone 10. Ht: 46cm (18in.). *Photo by Elizabeth Ellingson.*

Formulas for barium glaze (B) tile set 1

B27A: Dry Barium Blue – cone 10R (toxic)		B27B: Semi-dry Blue – cone 10R (toxic)		B27C: Satin Blue – cone 10R (toxic)	
Barium carb.	32	Barium carb.	34	Barium carb.	37.1
G22 spar	48	G22 spar	53	G22 spar	56.2
EPKaolin	20	EPKaolin	13	EPKaolin	6.7
	100		100		100
Copper carb.	3	Copper carb.	3	Copper carb.	3

B12: ML #7 – cone 10R (toxic)		B3A: Glaze 94 (J. DeBoos) – cone 10R (toxic)		B25A: (G. Daly) – cone 10R (toxic)	
Barium carb.	29.7	Spar	33.3	Nepheline syenite	12.5
Potash spar	29.7	Barium carb.	33.4	Dolomite	12.5
EPKaolin	30.2	Kaolin	33.3	Barium carb.	37.5
Silica	10.4		100	EPKaolin	37.5
	100	Copper carb.	3		100
Copper carb.	4			Cobalt carb.	1

B32: R3663B (J. Robinson) – cone 10R (toxic)		B33: R3663B (J. Robinson) – cone 10R (toxic)		B25B: (G. Daly) – cone 10R (toxic)	
Fusion frit 403	65	Fusion frit 403	65	Nepheline syenite	56
Nepheline syenite	10	Nepheline syenite	10	Dolomite	19
Alumina hydrate	25	Alumina hydrate	25	Barium carb.	19
	100		100	EPKaolin	6
Rutile	4	Copper carb.	5		100
Veegum	0.5	Veegum	0.5	Red iron oxide	10
				Nickel oxide	4

B4: 2824 Purple Matt (P. Horsley) – cone 6 (toxic)		B6B: Dry Turquoise – cone 6 (toxic)		B6: Dry Turquoise – cone 6 (toxic)	
Kingman spar	35	Nepheline syenite	48.3	Nepheline syenite	40
Fusion Frit 403	5	EPKaolin	24.2	Barium carb.	40
Barium carb.	40	Strontium carb.	27.5	EPKaolin	20
EPKaolin	18		100		100
C&C ball clay	2	Copper carb.	3	Copper carb.	5
	100				
Copper carb.	6				
Veegum	1.5				

Barium glaze (B) tile set 1 (*see formulas opposite*)

B16B: A.P. Matt #1 (A. Paul) – cone 6 (toxic)		B2B: Toxic Turquoise – cone 6 (toxic)		B2A: Toxic Turquoise – cone 6 (toxic)	
Nepheline syenite	26	Nepheline syenite	54	Nepheline syenite	54
Whiting	3	Barium carb.	32	Barium carb.	32
Barium carb.	27	EPKaolin	14	EPKaolin	14
Strontium carb.	12		100		100
EPKaolin	10	Cobalt carb.	2	Copper carb.	3
Silica	22				
	100				
Copper carb.	2				
B12C: Dry Matt – cone 6 (toxic)		**B12A: Barium Matt – cone 6 (toxic)**		**B14: R-1000 (from G. Gibson) – cone 6**	
Barium carb.	37.3	Barium carb.	30.5	Nepheline syenite	38.8
Potash spar	56	Potash spar	45.7	Wollastonite	15.3
EPKaolin	6.7	EPKaolin	12.1	Strontium carb.	15.3
	100	Silica	11.7	Gerstley borate	10.2
Copper carb.	3		100	EPKaolin	10.2
		Copper carb.	3	Silica	10.2
					100
B13A: R.S. Matte (from G. Gibson) – cone 6		**B13B: R.S. Matte (from G. Gibson) – cone 6**		**B15: Woo Satin Matt – cone 6 (toxic)**	
				F-4 spar	29
Nepheline syenite	60	Nepheline syenite	60	Barium carb.	21
Strontium carb.	22	Strontium carb.	22	Dolomite	10
Lithium carb.	5	Lithium carb.	5	EPKaolin	6
Ball clay	8	Ball clay	8	Silica	6
Silica	5	Silica	5	Frit 3195	16
	100		100	Ultrox	12
Copper carb.	2	Rutile	1.5		100
				Bentonite	2
				Manganese dioxide	2
				Cobalt carb.	0.5
B16A: A.P. Matt #1 – cone 6 (toxic)		**B5A: Pagan Purple – cone 6 (toxic)**		**B5D: Pagan Purple – cone 6 (toxic)**	
Nepheline syenite	26				
Whiting	3	Barium carb.	30	Barium carb.	30
Barium carb.	27	Lithium carb.	2.4	Lithium carb.	2.4
Strontium carb.	12	Zinc oxide	5.4	Zinc oxide	5.4
EPKaolin	10	Whiting	9.5	Whiting	9.5
Silica	22	Potash spar	36.4	Potash spar	36.4
	100	Silica	16.3	Silica	16.3
Bentonite	2		100		100
Chromium oxide	0.5	Nickel oxide	4	Copper carb.	6
Copper carb.	1				

Formulas for barium glaze (B) tile set 3

B36: Ford Green – cone 6 (toxic)		B37: Ford Yellow – cone 6 (toxic)		B38: Newcomb Blue – cone 6 (toxic)	
Barium carb.	39.2	Barium carb.	39.2	Nepheline syenite	50.3
Nepheline syenite	44.1	Nepheline syenite	44.1	Silica	8.3
Spodumene	9.8	Spodumene	9.8	Lithium carb.	1.2
Silica	4.9	Silica	4.9	Barium carb.	40.3
Bentonite	2	Bentonite	2		100
	100		100	Rutile	3.2
Red iron oxide	5	Rutile	20	Black copper oxide	4.1
Copper carb.	1				

B20: Blue-Green (J. Jernegan) – cone 3 (toxic)		B35: Varda's Blue Green – cone 04 (toxic)		B5B: Pagan Purple – cone 06 (toxic)	
Custer spar	42.1	Nepheline syenite	20.4	Barium carb.	30
Barium carb.	21.1	Strontium carb.	43.0	Lithium carb.	2.4
EPKaolin	5.3	Lithium carb.	5.4	Zinc oxide	5.4
Silica	10.5	Silica	10.8	Whiting	9.5
Gerstley borate	10.5	EPKaolin	20.4	Potash spar	36.4
Zinc oxide	10.5		100	Silica	16.3
	100	Copper carb.	7.5		100
Copper carb.	3			Chromium oxide	2

B5E: Pagan Purple – cone 06 (toxic)		B5A: Pagan Purple – cone 04 (toxic)		B5G: Pagan Purple – cone 06 (toxic)	
				Barium carb.	30
Barium carb.	30	Barium carb.	30	Lithium carb.	2.4
Lithium carb.	2.4	Lithium carb.	2.4	Zinc oxide	5.4
Zinc oxide	5.4	Zinc oxide	5.4	Whiting	9.5
Whiting	9.5	Whiting	9.5	Potash spar	36.4
Potash spar	36.4	Potash spar	36.4	Silica	16.3
Silica	16.3	Silica	16.3		100
	100		100	Iron chromate	2
Copper carb.	3	Nickel oxide	4	Copper carb.	4

B11E: PP Variants – cone 04 (toxic)		B11C: PP Variants – cone 04 (toxic)		B11A: PP Variants – cone 04 (toxic)	
Barium carb.	24.5	Barium carb.	32	Barium carb.	22.4
Potash spar	24.5	Potash spar	32	Potash spar	22.4
Lithium carb.	6.1	Lithium carb.	8	Lithium carb.	6.2
Zinc oxide	6.1	Zinc oxide	8	Zinc oxide	6.2
EPKaolin	16.2	EPKaolin	20	EPKaolin	21.4
Silica	22.6		100	Silica	21.4
	100	Black nickel oxide	2		100
Black nickel oxide	2			Black nickel oxide	2

Barium glaze (B) tile set 3 (see formulas opposite)

Formulas for barium glaze (B) tile set 4

B10: Dry Blue-Purple – cone 04 (toxic)		B21: Barium Base (S. Chamberlain) – cone 06 (toxic)		B24: Barium Variation (S. Chamberlain) – cone 06 (toxic)	
Barium carb.	43				
Nepheline syenite	20	Barium carb.	40	Barium carb.	43
EPKaolin	20	Lithium carb.	20	Lithium carb.	5.4
Lithium carb.	5	Nepheline syenite	20	Nepheline syenite	20.4
Silica	12	EPKaolin	20	EPKaolin	20.4
	100		100	Silica	10.8
Copper carb.	7	Copper carb.	2		100
				Copper carb.	3

B23: Barium Variation (S. Chamberlain) – cone 06 (toxic)		B22: Barium Base (S. Chamberlain) – cone 06 (toxic)		B24A: Barium Variation (S. Chamberlain) – cone 06 (toxic)	
Barium carb.	43				
Lithium carb.	5.4	Barium carb.	40	Strontium carb.	36.1
Nepheline syenite	20.4	Lithium carb.	20	Lithium carb.	6
EPKaolin	20.4	Nepheline syenite	20	Nepheline syenite	22.9
Silica	10.8	EPKaolin	20	EPKaolin	22.9
	100		100	Silica	12.1
Cobalt carb.	0.5	Red iron oxide	20		100
Chromium oxide	2			Copper carb.	3

B9: Chartreuse Crawl – cone 04 (toxic)		B7: Lana's Purple Aqua (L. Wilson) – cone 04 (toxic)		B17: Snow Base (from K. Finnerty) – cone 05 (toxic)	
Barium carb.	60	Barium carb.	47.9	Zinc oxide	13.3
Frit 3124	20	Nepheline syenite	47.9	Barium carb.	36.8
Silica	20	Frit 3134	4.2	Lithium carb.	8.8
	100		100	EPKaolin	14.5
Chromium oxide	1	Copper carb.	4	Silica	26.6
		Bentonite	2		100

B18: Topographical Base (from K. Finnerty) – cone 05 (toxic)		B8: Buddha's Juice (L. Wilson) – cone 04		B8B: Buddha's Juice (L. Wilson) – cone 04	
		Nepheline syenite	20	Nepheline syenite	20
Nepheline syenite	20	EPKaolin	20	EPKaolin	20
Barium carb.	40	Strontium carb.	36	Strontium carb.	36
Lithium carb.	20	Lithium carb.	6	Lithium carb.	6
EPKaolin	20	Silica	12	Silica	12
	100	Frit 3124	6	Frit 3124	6
			100		100
		Mason Stain 6236	20	Copper carb.	4

Hips and Hoar, John Chalke, 2008. Two cryolite (glaze) layers retaining their separate identities, with additions of chrome red (similar to BL14, p.76) added at a later firing. Fired to cone 04. W: 22cm (8¾in.). *Photo by Barbara Tipton.*

Chapter 9
Special effects glazes

If one visualises a smooth glossy transparent glaze as an ideal, then all deviations from that are considered flaws or defects. From that standpoint these textural and special-effects glazes represent serious defects, but within a broader context of fired surfaces on sculpture they are exciting possibilities to be explored. Such glazes suggest the transformations that ceramic materials go through in the process of firing, and contribute a distinctive character to the pieces.

The broken and varied surfaces are often visually active and add a complexity to the work, particularly in the case of 'shrink and crawl' glazes. Many of these glazes are sturdy and durable, but others are somewhat fragile compared to conventional smooth glazes: 'Shrink and crawl' glazes may chip or pieces may flake off when abraded or handled roughly; under direct pressure blistered or crater glazes can be crushed or new blisters can break open; very rough, dry surfaces may chip and be difficult to clean if subject to a lot of handling. It is important to test them and determine whether they are visually and physically suitable for the work on which they are to be used.

To better understand what creates these effects it makes sense to break them into the two main groups defined by the kinds of physical processes that create them.

'Shrink and crawl'

These are sometimes referred to as 'lizard skin' or 'leopard' glazes. This group of glaze effects occurs due to shrinkage of the glaze (or slip) coating during the drying and firing. When a smooth, wet coating is applied to the surface of a piece it shrinks somewhat as it dries. During the firing it often continues to shrink, pulling apart into many separate pieces. In a well-designed conventional glaze the amount of shrinkage is modest, and when the glaze melts it flows together into a smooth coating that gives no hint of what occurred during the firing. If the glaze does not smooth out or if there are bare patches of clay where the glaze has fallen off, the defect is known as 'crawling'.

This problem usually occurs in 'normal' glazes that have been applied too thickly and dried or fired too fast, exacerbating the shrinkage. It can also occur if the bisque surface is dusty or contaminated with oil or wax, interfering with the bond between the glaze and the clay. In 'shrink and crawl'-type glazes this process is exaggerated by the use of particular glaze materials and often thick application to encourage a high degree of shrinkage. Additionally, a dry or matt glaze is not fluid enough to flow back together during the firing, so the glaze surface is obviously broken and resembles a cracked lake bed. The visual effect of a 'shrink and crawl' glaze is much stronger if there is a significant value (light and dark) difference between the glaze and the surface beneath. For

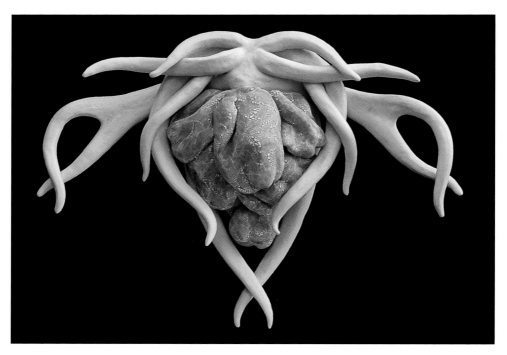

ABOVE *NurtureNature #2*, (detail, below) Bradley Sabin, 2002, Glazed with BL18 (p.74) on outer horn structure, and centre objects treated with red commercial underglaze beneath SE41 (p.116). Fired to cone 04. 46 × 41 × 12.5cm (18 × 16 × 5in.). *Photo by the artist.*

example, a dark crawl glaze is dramatic on a pale clay or slip, but rather subtle on a dark body. Firing a contrasting-colour slip, engobe or glaze on the ware before using a crawl glaze enhances the graphic effect. If a crawl glaze is fired well below its melting point, the surface may be sharp-edged and textural. If it is fired closer to the point of melting, the edges of the piece will soften to the point where the glaze may look more like spots than a crisply cracked surface – hence the term 'leopard glaze'.

The key factor in crawl glazes is a high shrinkage rate of the coating relative to the surface to which it is applied.

In most cases we are applying glaze to bisque-fired ware, so the clay does not shrink much more when fired to earthenware temperatures, and only moderately when fired to stoneware temperatures. One of the obvious but useful methods for creating this 'shrink and crawl' effect is to apply a slip with significant amounts of *raw clay* to a bisque- or glaze-fired surface. The shrinkage of the clay will cause it to pull apart and the surface will remain very dry. One problem with this approach is that slips do not usually have enough fluxing oxides to melt them onto the surface of the piece, and during or after the firing the slip may flake off. This problem can be solved by firing a semi-fluid glaze onto the piece first, and then applying the slip as a second layer and firing it again. The slip will shrink, but the pieces will be fused onto the surface of the fired glaze below (see Chapter 3, p.35). Many glazes contain some clay, which provides alumina and silica. Occasionally, the raw-clay content in a glaze may induce sufficient shrinkage to produce this effect. Alternatively, that effect can be exaggerated by substituting clay that shrinks more, such as ball clay or even bentonite, for a clay which shrinks less, such as kaolin.

By far the most common way to produce crawl glazes is with the use of one or two glaze materials that have a very high rate of shrinkage during the firing. *Magnesium carbonate* is a fluffy material that absorbs a large amount of water and shrinks considerably in the drying and firing (see Chapter 7). It is a popular choice for special-effect matt glazes because it is quite refractory at low temperatures and does not have too much of an effect on colour development. It is possible simply to add magnesium carbonate to an existing glaze in 10% increments and to note the shift toward greater shrinkage and often increased stiffness. Additions of 20–55% will cause noticeable crawling.

Lidded Jar, Richard Burkett, 2007. Glazed with SE35 (p.118) on bottom over a general coat of E28 (p.50). Soda-fired to cone 9. 28 × 12.5 × 12.5cm (11 × 5 × 5in.). *Photo by the artist.*

Cup with Improvised Handle, Richard Burkett, 1995. Stoneware, porcelain and steel. 10 × 18 × 8cm (4 × 7 × 3in.). *Photo by the artist.*

Maidenhair Box, Andi Moran, 2006. Glazed with SE38 (p.116) applied over glaze stain. Fired to cone 04. 48 × 23 × 12.5cm (19 × 9 × 5in.). *Photo by Tom Joynt.*

Zinc oxide also shrinks significantly during the firing and will reliably produce the same effect. Zinc is a somewhat more active flux than magnesium, but in high quantities it is also refractory and produces dry matt surfaces (see Chapter 6). However, it does have a strong and at times surprising effect on colouring oxides. Cobalt, for instance, turns dark green under the influence of zinc oxide. Zinc oxide is more likely to be used in a crawl glaze when the modification of colour is as important as the crawling effect.

There is another way to create a crawled surface that does not rely on the characteristics of the glaze materials, but rather the liquid medium it is mixed with for application. The organic gum CMC (sodium carboxymethylcellulose) is a useful and common material for suspending glaze materials and adding viscosity and 'brushability' to a glaze or engobe. It is sold as a powder that is mixed with water to produce a slimy thick liquid with a high rate of shrinkage upon drying and firing; I mix 200 g (7 oz) of CMC powder with 3 litres (*c.* 6$^{1}/_{2}$ pts) of hot water and allow it to absorb the water overnight. I have found that a well-screened dry, fritted glaze can be mixed with a thick mixture of CMC gum and some additional water and brushed or poured onto a piece. The glaze has a thick but liquid consistency similar to latex paint. The consistency may be varied, and with it the degree of crawling. The CMC gum causes the glaze to shrink and crawl in the early stages of the firing before it completely burns away. The glaze may need to be

Turquoise Knob Funnel, Virginia Scotchie, 2007. Glazed with variant of SE24 (p.118). Fired to cone 6. 91 × 48 × 43cm (36 × 19 × 17in.). *Photo by David Ramsey.*

fired to a lower than normal temperature to clearly show off the broken, crawled surface.

Crater, lava and foam glazes

During the melting process glazes go through a variety of stages, some of which are quite dramatic as the materials dissolve and interact. In many cases gases are liberated from the breakdown of compounds, and bubbles form in the viscous matrix of the melting glaze. The gases cause the mass to expand and swell, then collapse as bubbles pop and release the gas. More gases are generated, and the glaze swells, foams and bubbles until most of the gas is liberated and the glaze becomes fluid enough to lie flat on the surface of the clay in a smooth layer. This can be observed happening over the course of 15–20 minutes during a raku

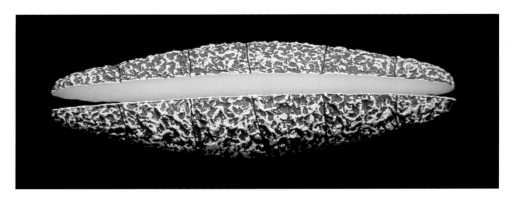

Untitled, Sally Brogden, 1992. Glazed with SE5 base glaze (p.121). Fired to cone 02. 71 × 23 × 10cm (28 × 9 × 4in.). *Photo by the artist.*

firing with a typical clear glaze based on gerstley borate and feldspar.

In this group of glazes, the process of melting and bubbling is typically arrested before the glaze can fully melt and smooth out.

The effects are traditionally known as bubbling, blistering or cratering depending on the size and type of 'flaw'. These are often fairly delicate surfaces because the bubbles may be easily broken open. The materials used in these glazes often are selected because they liberate large amounts of gas, ensuring a violent melting process and a resulting broken surface. Materials vary in the temperature at which the chemical decomposition occurs and the majority of gas is liberated. In this respect, varying the firing temperature can change the surface character of these glazes significantly. If fired hotter, they may melt out smoothly; whereas if the firing is cooler, they may not have begun the most active portion of the bubbling process. Shifting the conclusion of the firing, by as little as 20 degrees, to either earlier or later in the melting process can make a big difference. It is worthwhile to test these glazes at different temperatures to understand both the process and their potential. The most

common materials used in crater glazes include the following substances.

Cryolite (Na_3AlF_6) (see Chapter 5)
This is a source of sodium and alumina, and a powerful melting agent that liberates large amounts of fluorine gas when heated to mid-range and high temperatures. However, the gas is corrosive and may damage electric kiln elements as well as posing a danger in poorly ventilated kiln rooms. Because it generates so much gas, cryolite is rarely used outside of special-effect glazes.

Gerstley borate (colemanite) ($2CaO_3B_2O_3 5H_2O$) (see Chapter 6)
This is a widely used low-temperature flux that has a high loss-on-ignition. Approximately 25–30% of the weight is lost during the firing through the liberation of H_2O gas,[24] resulting in a boiling and foaming action, particularly in rapid firings like raku. It also has a relatively high rate of shrinkage due to the large quantity of water it absorbs in the glaze slop.

Bone ash ($Ca_3(PO_4)_2$) (see Chapter 7)
Bone ash is a moderately active flux made from calcined animal bones,

114

which decomposes under heat to liberate quantities of phosphorous oxide gas. Small amounts can result in pinholes and are responsible for the opalescence in Chun-type glazes. Large quantities can produce a broken surface.

Lithium carbonate (Li_2CO_3)(see Chapter 5)
This powerful low-temperature flux is a carbonate and liberates CO_2 gas when decomposing early in the firing.

Silicon carbide (SiC)

This is a manmade material that is used widely in kiln shelves and high-temperature refractories. When a powdered form is introduced into glazes it dissolves into the glaze melt, this process beginning at about $1832°F$ $(1000°C)$,[25] and disassociates into carbon and silicon. The melting process liberates large amounts of both carbon monoxide and carbon dioxide gas, which can cause a boiling and blistered surface in the glaze. When a blistered effect is desired, adding 3–8% of coarse (50–100 mesh) silicon carbide will usually be effective at mid to high temperatures (above cone 4). Silicon carbide may also be added to a slip or even the clay body to liberate gas so as to cause blistering in a covering glaze during the firing.

Toxicity and health concerns

Low to medium risk: The materials responsible for these glaze effects are not particularly toxic. Normal precautions should be taken to limit exposure to dusts containing silica and other materials. Cryolite liberates fluorine gas during the firing, so care should be taken to ventilate the kiln properly. These glazes are generally not suitable for any surfaces that come into contact with food or are required for utilitarian service such as floor tiles, basins, etc.

New Old Lace, John Chalke, 2008. Three layered glazes. Fired to cone 04. W: 23cm (9in.). *Photo by Barbara Tipton.*

SE8: Lichen (from B. Shay) – cone 04	
Magnesium carb.	35.7
Lithium carb.	7.1
Borax	35.7
Gerstley borate	21.5
	100
Copper carb.	2.9
Cobalt carb.	0.3

SE41: Valarians Sculpture White Beads (from B. Sabin) cone 06–04	
Borax	27
Magnesium carb.	33
Gerstley borate	33
Silica	7
	100
Zircopax	7

SE10: Messenger Crawl – cone 04	
Borax	3.88
Gerstley borate	46.5
Magnesium carb.	31
EPKaolin	18.6
	100
Zircopax	10

SE9: Shrink and Crawl #2 – cone 04	
Frit 3134	52.4
EPKaolin	23.8
Magnesium carb.	23.8
	100
Rutile	8

SE25B: Scotchie Beads (from A. Chabot) – cone 04	
Borax	26.7
Gerstley borate	33.3
Magnesium carb.	33.3
Silica	6.7
	100
Sky-blue stain	10

SE12: Mooncrackle (from K. Doherty) – cone 06	
Gerstley borate	14.3
Borax	28.6
Lithium carb.	7.1
EPKaolin	14.3
Magnesium carb.	35.7
	100

SE37: Crawling Dry Matt (from A. Moran) – cone 04	
Barium carb.	8.3
Gerstley borate	17.6
Magnesium carb.	26.9
Nepheline syenite	24.1
EPKaolin	14.8
Silica	8.3
	100

SE7B: Shrink and Crawl (J. Jernegan) – cone 06	
Zinc oxide	65
Gerstley borate	35
	100
Red iron oxide	6
Copper carb.	5
Cobalt carb.	3

SE7: Shrink and Crawl (J. Jernegan) – cone 06	
Zinc oxide	65
Gerstley borate	35
	100
Cobalt carb.	2

SE14: Lizard (from B. Shay) – cone 06	
Magnesium carb.	25
Gerstley borate	43.8
Nepheline syenite	12.5
Lithium carb.	9.4
Borax	6.3
Silica	3.0
	100
Chromium oxide	3

SE40: Shin Li's Good Crawl (from L. Duryea) – cone 04	
Frit 3124	50
EPKaolin	20
Magnesium carb.	30
	100
Cobalt oxide	1
Rutile	8
Copper carb.	4

SE38: Crawl (from A. Moran) – cone 04	
Borax	4
Gerstley borate	46
Magnesium carb.	31
EPKaolin	19
	100
Zircopax	5

Special effects (SE) glaze tile set 1 (*see formulas opposite*)

Formulas for special effects (SE) glaze tile set 2

SE24C: Textured Glaze (V. Scotchie) – cone 6		SE24B: Textured Glaze (V. Scotchie) – cone 6		SE36: Adriana's White Crawl (from A. Moran) – cone 04	
Bone ash	77.3	Bone ash	77.3	Bone ash	72.7
Cryolite	13.7	Cryolite	13.7	Cryolite	18.3
F-4 spar	8.6	F-4 spar	8.6	Gerstley borate	9
Barium carb.	0.4	Barium carb.	0.4		100
	100		100		
Cobalt carb.	3	Chromium oxide	2		

SE2: Blue Shrink and Crawl – cone 10R		SE35: Dry Crawl 3 (R. Burkett) – cone 6		SE4: Mark Bell Lichen Glaze – cone 6	
		Cryolite	8.5		
Nepheline syenite	45	Calcined kaolin	60.7	Soda spar	30
Magnesium carb.	55	EPKaolin	7.9	Magnesium carb.	31
	100	Whiting	6	Frit 25	6
Cobalt carb.	2	Magnesium carb.	15.4	Talc	8
		Silica	1.5	Zinc oxide	6
			100	EPKaolin	19
		Borax	5		100

SE1B: Blue Bead – cone 10R		E10 fired to cone 6, then E1A applied and re-fired to cone 6		SE41 applied over CO30 and fired once to cone 06	
Zinc oxide	60	*E10: Tim Mather's (modified) Iron Slip*		*SE41: Valarians White Beads*	
Whiting	20	Slip clay (Alberta)	37	Borax	27
EPKaolin	20	Custer spar	18	Magnesium carb.	33
	100	Wood ash	18	Gerstley borate	33
Cobalt carb.	2	Red iron oxide	27	Silica	7
		E1A: Modified White Slip (J. Jernegan)			100
		EPKaolin	25	Zircopax	7
		Ball clay	35	*CO30: Ted's Black (T. Vogel)*	
		Silica	15	Mason Stain 6600	44.4
		Potash spar	25	Gerstley borate	44.4
			100	Black copper oxide	11.2
		Zircopax	10		100
		Bentonite	5		

SE33: Kim's Dry Crawl – cone 6		CO27 – cone 10R (toxic)		SE26: Lizard Skin – cone 04	
				Frit 3134	55
		Custer spar	53	Talc	16.5
Custer spar	27	Manganese dioxide	21	Dolomite	17.2
EPKaolin	9	Alberta slip clay	13	EPKaolin	6.3
Whiting	12.9	Copper carb.	11	Silica	5
Silica	14.9	Cobalt oxide	2		100
Gerstley borate	13.1		100		
Magnesium carb.	23.1	Silicon carbide (50 mesh)	3	Silicon carbide (50 mesh)	0.6
	100			Bentonite	0.5
Silicon carbide (50 mesh) 30.8				Copper carb.	3
				Black nickel oxide	2

Special effects (SE) glaze tile set 2 (*see formulas opposite*)

Formulas for special effects (SE) glaze tile set 3

SE5C: Moss Base (S. Brogden) – cone 02		SE5A: Moss Base (S. Brogden) – cone 02		SE19: Weirdo Foam (B. Sabin) – cone 06	
Cryolite	43	Cryolite	43	Frit 3110	50
Whiting	15	Whiting	15	Bone ash	40
EPKaolin	21	EPKaolin	21	Ball clay	10
Silica	21	Silica	21		100
	100		100		
Ilmenite	8	Bentonite	2		
Copper carb.	2	Manganese dioxide	2		

SE23: Rick's Dry Original (from S. Brogden) – cone 04		SE16: Black Lava Glaze (J. Jernegan) – cone 013		SE32: Erich's Crusty Cream (E. Winzer) – cone 04 (toxic)	
Cryolite	22.3	Frit 3124	75	Cryolite	50
Lithium carb.	4	Gerstley borate	25	Lithium carb.	50
EPKaolin	11		100		100
Whiting	16.1	Mason stain 6600	10		
Silica	46.6				
	100				
Chromium oxide	0.5				
Ultrox	10				

SE3: Cryolite #1 – cone 6		SE21A: Chalke Glaze II (J. Chalke) – cone 6		SE21: Chalke Glaze II (J. Chalke) – cone 6	
Barium carb.	5.7				
Gerstley borate	5.7	Cryolite	50	Cryolite	50
Talc	14.3	Talc	50	Talc	50
Cryolite	74.3		100		100
	100	Zircopax	10	Copper carb.	3
Cobalt carb.	0.25	Rutile	3		
Rutile	2.0				
Zircopax	16.0				

SE18A: Chalke Wild Rose (J. Chalke) – cone 6		SE18B: Chalke Wild Rose (J. Chalke) Variant – cone 6		SE22: Rick's Dry Version II (from S. Brogden) – cone 04	
				Cryolite	18
				Custer spar	9
Lithium carb.	10.5	Lithium carb.	10.5	Lithium carb.	2
Bone ash	10.5	Bone ash	10.5	EPKaolin	16
Nepheline syenite	61.5	Nepheline syenite	61.5	Flourspar	10
EPKaolin	17.5	EPKaolin	17.5	Silica	45
	100		100		100
Chromium oxide	0.5	Rutile	10	Chromium oxide	0.5
Cryolite	5			Ultrox	10

Special effects (SE) glaze tile set 3 (*see formulas opposite*)

Passage, Ted Vogel, 2005. 76 × 46 × 30cm (30 × 18 × 12in.). The birds are CO30 (p.134), the trunk is black copper oxide under a Redart sigillata (see E20, p.52), and the thumbprint is copper-oxide wash applied and wiped off. Fired to cone 04. *Photo by Bill Bachhuber.*

Chapter 10

Colouring oxides and raku-fired matts

Colouring oxides

All the materials we use in glazes are made up of elements bonded to oxygen, and thus may be referred to as 'oxides' (though some are carbonates or other combinations of oxygen and hydrogen and carbon). This is particularly true of the fluxing metallic oxides like lead or zinc, but it also includes the alkalis and the alkaline earth metals such as barium, calcium and strontium. These oxides are primarily used to promote melting in a glaze, and in proper balance will dissolve into a colourless glass. However, a reference to an 'oxide wash' or 'colouring oxides' means the metallic oxides – cobalt, chrome, copper, iron, rutile, etc. – that are normally used to colour the glaze.

These oxides are typically used in small quantities, from 0.25%–5% in the case of cobalt, to 2%–10% in the case of iron. The common convention for writing a glaze, which is followed in this book (see the Introduction), reflects the presumption

Avocado Bronze Bowl, Virginia Scotchie, 2005. Glazed with CO1A (p.134) (bronze sections) and SE24B (p.118) applied very thickly. Fired to cone 6. 36 × 56 × 33cm (14 × 22 × 13in.). *Photo by David Ramsey.*

that the glaze base is a complete formula, and the colouring oxide(s) is added on top of it to colour the glaze to taste. While this is a reasonable premise in a conventional glaze, there are considerable opportunities to develop surface treatments that turn this ratio upside down, and these are based primarily on the colouring oxides themselves. Such 'oxide wash' surfaces tend to be quite dark, matt and opaque, though also quite thin. Because there is very little glaze body to them, they do not cover the surface texture of the clay very much, and thus they can be very useful in preserving or enhancing subtle surface textures.

Oxide washes that are applied to bisque ware and then selectively wiped away are probably the most direct and effective way to turn surface texture into a graphic visual experience. Sometimes called 'body stains', they are very easy to mix and can be used under or over engobes, slips or glazes in a variety of ways (see Chapter 3, pp. 32–34). Heavy application of raw oxide wash may cause a glaze applied over it to crawl or pull away if the oxide coating is not partially wiped off first. In some cases colouring oxide mixtures may be applied fairly heavily, resulting in a melted surface that slightly resembles a silica-based glaze but has a dense metallic character. Oxide washes are strong colourants, so they are typically suspended in thin mixture with water. The formulas given show a particular ratio as tested, but most artists mix by eye. An addition of CMC or other gum will help keep the oxides in suspension longer.

Also included in this chapter are glazes that are very high in colouring oxides but which also contain supplemental fluxing and glass-forming oxides. These glazes tend to be near black and have a strong metallic character.

Cobalt oxide (CoO) (toxic)

Cobalt is familiar for producing very strong blue hues in slips and glazes. As a pure oxide it is very refractory, with a melting point of 2860°C (5180°F). The carbonate form ($CoCO_3$) is about half the strength, but still produces very strong blue-black tones when applied to bare clay. At earthenware temperatures pure cobalt dusts off and requires a little fritted flux to fuse it on. At stoneware temperatures it fuses to most clay bodies, and may develop a slight sheen. It does not react significantly with slips or engobes over it, but will strongly colour any fused glaze surface it is in contact with.

Copper oxide (CuO) (toxic)

Black copper oxide or the less-concentrated copper carbonate is a favourite metallic oxide because it has a relatively low melting point, 1148°C (2098°F), and is very reactive and volatile. As low as cone 04 it melts into a fused brown-black surface on clay, and can also be used at stoneware temperature, though thick applications will run. It interacts readily with engobes or glazes applied over it at earthenware temperatures and higher, creating brown to green staining effects that have an irregular and soft edge, and may develop reds in reduction firings (see Chapter 3, pp. 33–4).

Chrome oxide (CrO) (toxic)

Chrome oxide produces strong green hues in glazes under most circumstances, but may also produce yellow, reds and oranges in lead glazes at low temperatures. Pure chromium oxide is not useful as an oxide wash because it is very refractory, with a melting point of 2265°C (4109°F); even mixed with fritted fluxes it tends to powder off.

However, two other types of chrome do work in wash forms.

Iron chromate (FeCrO₃) is a naturally occurring blend of iron and chromium, is useful for developing grey tones in glazes, and as an oxide wash is close to a true black colour. The melting point is 1700°C (3092°F), but it will fuse onto clay at stoneware temperatures. It may also be used at earthenware temperatures with the addition of 25% frit 3124, and produces a black colour.

Potassium dichromate (K₂Cr₂O₇) is a bright-orange crystalline compound combining chromium with potassium. It is soluble in water and very toxic. It is used at low temperatures to develop red glazes with a leaded frit, and its melting point is low enough that it will produce a transparent green tone on clay surfaces at stoneware temperatures. With the addition of up to 20% fritted flux it will also work at earthenware temperatures. Heavy applications of the undissolved crystal compound will melt into a glassy glaze.

Red iron oxide (Fe₂O₃)
This is the oxidised form of iron and is commonly used both for colouring glazes and as an oxide wash. It is relatively non-toxic, inexpensive and versatile. Interestingly, red iron has a higher melting point, 1565°C (2849°F), than the reduced form, black iron oxide (FeO), which melts at 1420°C (2588°F).²⁶ Iron oxide needs to be mixed with a small amount of flux to adhere to clay surfaces at earthenware temperatures, but fuses readily to most clay bodies at stoneware temperatures. Though a fairly strong colourant, iron does not fume or volatilise to any significant degree. There are several other common forms of iron,

Brute Boxes (detail), Andi Moran, 2006. Glazed with SE36 (p.118) applied over CO28 (p.134) and fired to cone 04. *Photo by Tom Joynt.*

including yellow ochre (Fe₂O₃ 3H₂O), which is less strong, though in firing they all oxidise to the red iron form at temperatures above 900°C (1652°F), and can all be reduced to the black iron form. Slip clays like Barnard or Alberta are rich in iron (as are red earthenware clays like Redart) and can also be used as body stains. When used as a surface wash, iron tends to produce red-browns at earthenware temperatures, and dark browns at stoneware temperatures. Reduction firings do not produce black because the iron reoxidises partially upon cooling, the exception being when particular care is taken to fire down the kiln, a reducing atmosphere being maintained until the ware is below about 870°C (1598°F). Iron mixes well with rutile (see below), producing more gold-brown hues when mixed in equal parts.

Manganese oxide (MnO) (toxic)
This is usually introduced as the common manganese dioxide (MnO₂),

Brute Boxes, Andi Moran, 2006. Glazed with SE36 (p.118) applied over CO28 (p.134) and fired to cone 04. Approx. 20 × 25cm (8 × 10in.) each. *Photo by Tom Joynt.*

and is a fairly active metal oxide, particularly at high temperatures. Its melting point is listed as 1650°C (3002°F), but in interaction with clay bodies and other materials it melts readily above 1150°C (2102°F).[27] At stoneware temperatures it produces a satin-black metallic surface with some beading where thick. A popular quasi-glaze combines 80% manganese dioxide with 10% copper carbonate and 10% kaolin, to produce a remarkable bronze-like surface at cone 6 (CO1A, p.134). Because the dioxide decomposes to monoxide at 1080°C (1976°F) and liberates gas, a bubbled or blistered surface can result. At earthenware temperatures a fritted flux is needed to help it adhere to the ceramic surface, and brown-black tones result, (see tiles CO1B, CO1C, p.134). Additional flux produces gunmetal metallic surfaces.

Nickel oxide (NiO) (toxic)
This is used in both the black oxide and the green nickel carbonate ($NiCO_3$) forms. It is quite refractory, with a melting point of 1990°C (3614°F), and not suitable as an oxide wash because it resists fusing and powders off even with added frit.

Rutile (TiO_2)
This is a naturally occurring form of titanium dioxide mixed with up to 15% iron impurities. Rutile is quite refractory in practice, with a melting point of 1825°C (3317°F). In stoneware glazes titanium dissolves completely during the melting process, but readily recrystallises on cooling. Rutile and pure titanium dioxide are very useful for developing micro and macrocrystalline glazes (see Chapter 1, p.13). At earthenware temperatures rutile is difficult to dissolve and tends to cause matting. As an oxide wash it will fuse to form a warm orange-brown surface, but it needs to be mixed with a fritted flux to adhere to ceramic surfaces at all but the highest temperatures.

Titanium dioxide (TiO_2) has a slightly higher melting point but will also work as an oxide wash with the addition of a fluxing frit like 3124. At stoneware temperatures it results in an orange-tan colour, and at earthenware temperatures it is a pale cream. The mixture of red iron oxide, rutile and nepheline syenite or gerstley borate in three equal parts is a popular decorating wash that works very well as body stain for producing an orange-gold to brown colour.

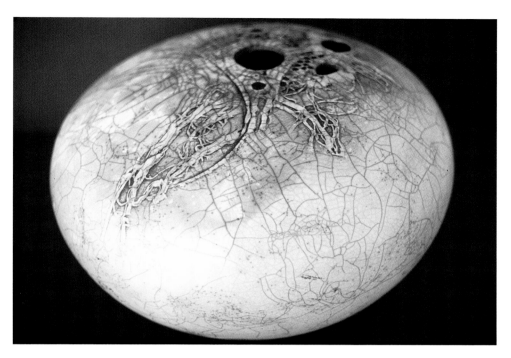

Untitled, David Kuraoka, 1975. Porcelain slip over stoneware, glazed with CO18 (p.132) raku-fired with post-firing reduction. 4 × 8 × 8cm (10 × 20 × 20in.). *Photo by the artist.*

Toxicity and health concerns

High to low risk: Metallic colouring oxides range from relatively inert materials like rutile and iron oxides, to the highly toxic oxides of chromium, nickel, manganese and copper, so real care must be taken when handling them. These are quite concentrated materials which are usually present in glazes in small amounts, and can pose an acute toxicity hazard. Breathing the dust should be avoided when mixing, and wearing protective gloves and an apron is recommended to avoid unnecessary contact with the skin, particularly when applying to and wiping off surfaces.

American raku

The raku-firing process began in the 16th century in Japan, where it has continued to be practised by the Raku family potters. It was and is primarily based on modestly sized ware made for the tea ceremony, produced through a rapid firing process usually concluded by removing the ware from the kiln during the height of the firing. The American ceramic artist Paul Soldner is largely credited with popularising the fast-firing earthenware process during the 1960s, and adding a post-firing reduction step after the ware is removed from the kiln. Known as American raku, this process develops a particular marking and glaze reduction that the Japanese ware does not possess.

The raku-firing process involves loading glazed pieces into a special fast-firing kiln and heating them up to the maturing temperature of roughly cone 06, or 1013°C (1855°F), over the course of about an hour, verifying that the glazes are melted by observing them (or by using a pyrometric cone) and then shutting off the kiln. At this point the ware is typically removed with tongs and placed in contact with paper, straw or other combustible material, which catches fire and produces smoke. The ware and burning material is then covered with a steel can, trapping the smoke and allowing the ware to cool in a carbon-rich atmosphere. This type of post-firing reduction results in a variety of effects, including the charging of any unglazed clay with carbon, which results in a black or grey body. Perhaps the most dramatic effect is the reduction of copper oxide to the metallic form, which can result in an oil-on-water-type iridescent lustre finish. Reduced copper oxide may produce a range of hues, from orange-red to purple through to a polished metallic copper colour.

The original Japanese raku glazes were primarily lead-based glassy surfaces, and were coloured with iron and probably slip clays to produce a black glaze and an iron-red glaze. By the 1970s most raku glazes were based on gerstley borate, borax, low-melting frits and feldspar in various proportions. A simple and popular raku clear base is 60% gerstley borate and 40% potash feldspar. Adding 2–5% copper carbonate will produce lustre effects in cooling reduction. This type of transparent glaze is often called a crackle glaze. In fact the glaze fit phenomenon of crazing or crackling is common in many earthenware glazes (see Chapter 5, p.58). What makes it a dramatic feature in the raku process is the way the free carbon penetrates the crack lines and emphasises them.

Because the maximum temperature in raku-firing is often determined by watching the glazes melt, it is easy to halt the firing early and shift a glaze surface from glossy to a partially melted matt. Most glossy raku glazes can be easily under-fired to produce a drier surface. David Kuraoka, a well-known ceramic artist in San Francisco, developed dramatic crackle effects on sculptural raku forms, with a thick layer of white slip beneath a slightly under-fired clear matt glaze (see image p.127). The thermal shock of the firing caused the slip to develop long fine cracks which were darkened with the carbon from the reduction process. The matt surface of the glaze emphasised the form and the nuanced surface.

While originally a special palette of glazes was used for the raku-firing process, often featuring copper oxides, most earthenware glazes that fire in the cone 06 range will work. Heavy reduction may make non-copper-bearing glazes look overly dark and murky, so lighter reduction is often better. The glaze tile samples illustrate the same glazes fired with and without post-firing reduction. The simplicity of many raku glazes and the rapidity of the raku-firing process has encouraged wide experimentation with glaze compositions and produced some very interesting results in quite unorthodox glazes. Flux-saturated matts are common, as are sintered matts. Interestingly, copper will reduce to a red or metallic surface even in glazes that are not melted to a significant degree.

The intense colour response from a dry surface can be quite dramatic. In some cases, however, these glazes are susceptible to reoxidising over a period of weeks or months. This occurs when there is insufficient glass to seal the surface and the metallic copper is exposed to oxygen in the air and slowly reverts to a partially oxidised form, losing some of the colour it had after the firing (metallic copper or a tone from red through to purple).

Finally, the post-firing reduction process may be controlled to a greater degree than one might think. Four primary factors influence the result of the smoking process. The first is how hot the work was fired (use a cone to verify this), and the second is how long it cooled after the kiln was turned off, before it was placed in a reducing environment (time it approximately). The third factor is how much reduction material was used (newspaper sheets can be counted and shredded), and the fourth is how large the reduction chamber is and how tightly it contains the smoke. For instance, I fired the first of two test tiles (CO22, p.136) to cone 05, lifted off the raku kiln top and allowed the tiles to cool for 30 seconds. They were then placed on a bed of shredded paper (four sheets), which burned for 15 seconds, before being tightly covered with a 40 litre (10 gallon) washtub and allowed to cool for 30 minutes. The other tile (using the identical CO22 recipe) was allowed to cool for 60 seconds before reduction, and the results are partially oxidised greens and oranges instead of metallic tones. By quantifying these variables and observing the differences, you can reliably reproduce reduction effects.

Toxicity and health concerns

Medium risk: While many raku-glaze bases are not strictly toxic, they may contain copper or other metal oxides, sometimes in large amounts. Copper is a poisonous metal, so care should be taken

Untitled, Joy Ricciardi, 1982. Multiple raku firings with post-firing reduction. 46 × 25 × 18cm (18 × 10 × 7in.). *Photo by Doug DeFor.*

when handling such glazes. They should not be used for surfaces that come into contact with food. Some raku glazes contain large amounts of borax or soda ash, which are caustic and may irritate the skin. Breathing the dust should be avoided when mixing, and wearing protective gloves and an apron is recommended so as to avoid unnecessary contact with the skin. Moreover, the post-firing reduction process exposes the artist to smoke, which may contain a variety of compounds that can injure the lungs. The firing process should be conducted outside or with powerful ventilation, so as to dissipate or remove smoke and fumes as rapidly as possible.

Formulas for colouring oxide and raku glaze (CO) tile set 1

CO3: Cobalt Carbonate Wash – cone 04 (toxic). Left side wiped off	CO4: Red Iron Oxide Wash – cone 04. Left side wiped off	CO2: Copper Carbonate Wash –cone 04 (toxic). Left side wiped off
Cobalt carb. 100 g Gerstley borate 6 g Water 6 cups (1.4 l) Add CMC gum as needed to aid in suspension.	Red iron oxide 50 g Rutile 50 g Gerstley borate 15 g Nepheline syenite 15 g Water 2 cups (0.47 l) Add CMC gum as needed to aid in suspension.	Copper carb. 100 g Water 2 cups (0.47 l) Add CMC gum as needed to aid in suspension.
CO16A: Manganese Dioxide Wash – cone 04 (toxic)	**CO21A: Titanium Dioxide Wash – cone 04**	**CO14A: Rutile Wash – cone 04**
Manganese dioxide 50 g Frit 3124 20 g Water 1 cup (0.24 l) Add CMC gum as needed to aid in suspension.	Titanium dioxide 50 g Frit 3124 20 g Water 1 cup (0.24 l) Add CMC gum as needed to aid in suspension.	Rutile 50 g Frit 3124 20 g Water 1 cup (0.24 l) Add CMC gum as needed to aid in suspension.
CO12C: Iron Chromate Wash – cone 10R (toxic)	**CO15C: Potassium Dichromate Wash – cone 10R (toxic)**	**CO3: Cobalt Carbonate Wash – cone 10R (toxic)**
Iron chromate 50 g Water 1 cup (0.24 l) Add CMC gum as needed to aid in suspension.	Potassium dichromate 50 g Water 1 cup (0.24 l) Add CMC gum as needed to aid in suspension.	Cobalt carb. 100 g Gerstley borate 6 g Water 6 cups (1.4 l) Add CMC gum as needed to aid in suspension.
CO21C: Titanium Dioxide Wash – cone 10R	**CO14C: Rutile Wash – cone 10R**	**CO4: Red Iron Oxide Wash – cone 10R**
Titanium dioxide 50 g Frit 3124 10 g Water 1 cup (0.24 l) Add CMC gum as needed to aid in suspension.	Rutile 50 g Frit 3124 15 g Water 1 cup (0.24 l) Add CMC gum as needed to aid in suspension.	Red iron oxide 50 g Rutile 50 g Gerstley borate 15 g Nepheline syenite 15 g Water 2 cups (0.47 l) Add CMC gum as needed to aid in suspension.

Formulas for colouring oxide and raku glaze (CO) tile set 2

CO18: Kuraoka Clear Matt (D. Kuraoka) – cone 010 with light post-firing reduction (PFR)		A3: Turquoise Suede (J. Jernegan) – cone 06 oxidation (toxic)		A3: Turquoise Suede (J. Jernegan) – cone 06 with moderate PFR (toxic)	
		Lithium carb.	28.1	Lithium carb.	28.1
Gerstley borate	50	EPKaolin	10.4	EPKaolin	10.4
Nepheline syenite	50	Calcined kaolin	20.8	Calcined kaolin	20.8
	100	Bentonite	5.2	Bentonite	5.2
		Silica	35.5	Silica	35.5
			100		100
		Copper carb.	4	Copper carb.	4
CO22: Lithium Raku II (J. Jernegan) – cone 05 with light PFR (toxic)		**CO9A: Dry Lithium Raku** (A. Hirondelle) – cone 06 oxidation (toxic)		**CO9A: Dry Lithium Raku** (A. Hirondelle) – cone 06 with moderate PFR (toxic)	
Lithium carb.	70	Silica	54	Silica	54
Borax	10	Lithium carb.	29.4	Lithium carb.	29.4
Bentonite	15	EPKaolin	13.7	EPKaolin	13.7
Cornwall stone	5	Bentonite	2.9	Bentonite	2.9
	100		100		100
Black copper oxide	10	Red iron oxide	1	Red iron oxide	1
		Cobalt carb.	0.24	Cobalt carb.	0.24
CO9D: Dry Lithium Raku (A. Hirondelle) – cone 06 oxidation (toxic)		**CO9B: Dry Lithium Raku** (A. Hirondelle) – cone 06 oxidation (toxic)		**CO9B: Dry Lithium Raku** (A. Hirondelle) – cone 06 with moderate PFR (toxic)	
Silica	54	Silica	54	Silica	54
Lithium carb.	29.4	Lithium carb.	29.4	Lithium carb.	29.4
EPKaolin	13.7	EPKaolin	13.7	EPKaolin	13.7
Bentonite	2.9	Bentonite	2.9	Bentonite	2.9
	100		100		100
Rutile	4	Ochre	4	Ochre	4
Copper carb.	0.5	Red iron oxide	2	Red iron oxide	2
CO9D: Dry Lithium Raku (A. Hirondelle) – cone 06 with moderate PFR (toxic)		**CO9C: Dry Lithium Raku** (A. Hirondelle) – cone 06 oxidation (toxic)		**CO9C: Dry Lithium Raku** (A. Hirondelle) – cone 06 with moderate PFR (toxic)	
Silica	54	Silica	54	Silica	54
Lithium carb.	29.4	Lithium carb.	29.4	Lithium carb.	29.4
EPKaolin	13.7	EPKaolin	13.7	EPKaolin	13.7
Bentonite	2.9	Bentonite	2.9	Bentonite	2.9
	100		100		100
Rutile	4	Manganese dioxide	4	Manganese dioxide	4
Copper carb.	0.5	Cobalt carb.	1	Cobalt carb.	1

Colouring oxide and raku glaze (CO) tile set 2 (*see formulas opposite*)

Formulas for colouring oxide and raku glaze (CO) tile set 3

CO1A: Bronze Gold Metallic – cone 6 (toxic)		CO1B: Bronze Variant – cone 2 (toxic)		CO1C: Bronze Variant – cone 06 (toxic)	
Manganese dioxide	81.8	Manganese dioxide	69.2	Manganese dioxide	56
Copper carb.	9.1	Copper carb.	7.7	Copper carb.	6.3
EPKaolin	9.1	EPKaolin	7.7	EPKaolin	6.4
	100	Nepheline syenite	7.7	Nepheline syenite	6.3
		Frit 3134	7.7	Frit 3134	25
			100		100

CO25: #78 (J. Conrad) – cone 10R (toxic)		CO26: #361 (J. Conrad) – cone 10R (toxic)		CO24: #363 (J. Conrad) – cone 10R (toxic)	
Manganese dioxide	40	Custer spar	53	Custer spar	49.5
Copper oxide	30	Manganese dioxide	21	Manganese dioxide	23.2
Ball clay	30	Alberta slip clay	13	Alberta slip clay	17.2
	100	Copper carb.	11	Copper carb.	7.1
		Cobalt oxide	2	Cobalt oxide	3
			100		100

CO19: Dark Brown Wash (V. Cushing) – cone 10R (toxic)		CO16C: Manganese Dioxide Wash – cone 10R (toxic)		CO20: Black Wash (V. Cushing) – cone 10R (toxic)	
		Manganese dioxide	50 g		
Red iron oxide	40	Water	1 cup (0.24 l)	Redart clay	30
Manganese dioxide	30			Calcined kaolin	20
Ferro frit 3124	30	Add CMC gum as needed to		Frit 3124	20
	100	aid in suspension.		Manganese dioxide	10
				Red iron oxide	15
				Cobalt carb.	5
					100

CO28: Bronze (from A. Moran) – cone 04 (toxic)		CO29: J's Black (from A. Moran) – cone 04 (toxic)		CO30: Ted's Black (T. Vogel) – cone 03 (toxic)	
Lithium carb.	3	Custer spar	26.2		
Whiting	10.2	Frit 3124	17.4	Mason stain 6600	44.4
Frit 3124	12	Whiting	8.7	Gerstley borate	44.4
Ball clay	22.8	Red iron oxide	20.3	Black copper oxide	11.2
Silica	12	Cobalt carb.	7		100
Black copper oxide	9	Copper carb.	11.6		
Manganese dioxide	30	Manganese dioxide	3		
CMC gum	1	Bentonite	5.8		
	100		100		

Colouring oxide and raku glaze (CO) tile set 3 (*see formulas opposite*)

Formulas for colouring oxide and raku glaze (CO) tile set 4

CO8: Dry Alligator/Red Rust Raku (R. Pipenburg) – cone 06 with heavy PFR (toxic)		CO11B: Copper Sand – cone 06 oxidation (toxic)		CO11B: Copper Sand – cone 06 with moderate PFR (toxic)	
Gerstley borate	57.1	Gerstley borate	80	Gerstley borate	80
Nepheline syenite	14.3	Bone ash	20	Bone ash	20
Bone ash	28.6		100		100
	100	Copper carb.	5	Copper carb.	5
Copper carb.	10	Cobalt oxide	2.5	Cobalt oxide	2.5
		Tin oxide	1.5	Tin oxide	1.5

CO8: Dry Alligator/Red Rust Raku (R. Pipenburg) – cone 06 oxidation (toxic)		CO7: Weiser's Rust – cone 06 oxidation (toxic)		CO7: Weiser's Rust – cone 06 with moderate PFR (toxic)	
Gerstley borate	57.1	Gerstley borate	53.8	Gerstley borate	53.8
Nepheline syenite	14.3	Nepheline syenite	18.6	Nepheline syenite	18.6
Bone ash	28.6	Copper carb.	17.8	Copper carb.	17.8
	100	Black nickel oxide	4.9	Black nickel oxide	4.9
Copper carb.	10	Tin oxide	4.9	Tin oxide	4.9
			100		100

CO6: Crusty Copper (J. Jernegan) – cone 06 oxidation (toxic)		CO5: Soldner's Halo Wash (P. Soldner) – cone 06 oxidation (toxic)		CO5: Soldner's Halo Wash (P. Soldner) – cone 06 with heavy PFR (toxic)	
Borax	33	Gerstley borate	14	Gerstley borate	14
Gerstley borate	34	EPKaolin	57	EPKaolin	57
EPKaolin	33	Silica	29	Silica	29
	100		100		100
Copper carb.	15	Red iron oxide	50	Red iron oxide	50
Nickel carb.	15	Copper oxide	50	Copper oxide	50

CO6: Crusty Copper (J. Jernegan) – cone 06 with heavy PFR (toxic)		CO22: Lithium Raku II (J. Jernegan) – cone 05 oxidation (toxic)		CO22: Lithium Raku II (J. Jernegan) – cone 05 with moderate PFR (toxic)	
Borax	33	Lithium carb.	70	Lithium carb.	70
Gerstley borate	34	Borax	10	Borax	10
EPKaolin	33	Bentonite	15	Bentonite	15
	100	Cornwall stone	5	Cornwall stone	5
Copper carb.	15		100		100
Nickel carb.	15	Black copper oxide	10	Black copper oxide	10

References

1   Parmalee, C. W. *Ceramic Glazes*, (2nd edn), (Industrial Publications, 1951), p. 88
2   Parmalee, 89
3   Eppler, Richard A. and Eppler, Douglas R., *Glazes and Glass Coatings*, American Ceramic Society, 2000) p. 7
4   Rhodes, Daniel, *Clay and Glazes For the Potter*, (rev. edn) (Chilton, 1973) p. 74
5   Seger, Herman A., Collected Writings, (Vol 2), (Chemical Publishing, 1902); p. 566
6   Parmalee, 94
7   Coffey, Neil, French – English Dictionary, www.french-linguistics.co.uk/ dictionary/ 2009
8   Hamer, Frank and Janet, *The Potter's Dictionary of Materials and Techniques*, Revised Edition, (Watson-Guptill 1986), p. 5
9   Hamer, 361–363.
10 Richard A Eppler and Douglas R Eppler, *Glazes and Glass Coatings*, American Ceramic Society, 2000) p. 251.
11 Richard A Eppler and Douglas R Eppler, *Glazes and Glass Coatings*, American Ceramic Society, 2000) p. 22.
12 Parmalee, C. W. *Ceramic Glazes*, (2nd edn), (Industrial Publications, 1951), p. 24
13 Hansen, Tony, Ceramic Materials. Info/ Ceramic Oxides Database, DigitalFire Corporation, http://ceramic-materials.com zinc oxide
14 Parmalee, C. W. *Ceramic Glazes*, (2nd edn), (Industrial Publications, 1951), p. 18
15 Parmalee, 18
16 Hansen, Tony, *Ceramic Materials*. Info/ Ceramic Oxides Database, DigitalFire Corporation (www.ceramic-materials.com Calcium Oxide)
17 Parmalee, C. W. *Ceramic Glazes*, (2nd edn), (Industrial Publications, 1951), p. 18
18 Hamer, Frank and Janet, *The Potter's Dictionary of Materials and Techniques*, Revised Edition, (Watson-Guptill 1986) p. 118
19 Eppler, Richard A. and Eppler, Douglas R., *Glazes and Glass Coatings*, American Ceramic Society, 2000), p. 31.
20 Charles McKee, *Ceramic Handbook: A Guide to Glaze Calculation, Materials and Processes* (Star Publishing, 1984), p. 16
21 Eppler, 64
22 Frank and Janet Hamer, *The Potter's Dictionary of Materials and Techniques*, (rev. edn), (Watson-Guptill 1986), p. 306
23 John Britt, *The Complete Guide to High Fire Glazes* (Lark Books, 2007), p.20
24 Tony Hansen, Ceramic Materials. Info / Ceramic Oxides Database, DigitalFire Corporation, (http://digitalfire.com/gerstley borate/description.html)
25 Hamer, Frank and Janet, *The Potter's Dictionary of Materials and Techniques*, (rev. edn), (Watson-Guptill, 1986), p. 88.
26 Hamer, Frank and Janet, *The Potter's Dictionary of Materials and Techniques*, (rev. edn), (Watson-Guptill, 1986), p.175.
27 Hamer, 209

Bibliography

Britt, John, *The Complete Guide to High Fire Glazes* (Lark Books, 2007).

Clark, Nancy, Cutter, Thomas & McGrane, Jean-Anne, *Ventilation: A practical guide for artists, craftspeople and others in the arts* (Lyons Books, 1984).

Currie, Ian, *Revealing Glazes Using the Grid Method* (Bootstrap Press, 2002).

Daly, Greg, *Glazes and Glazing Techniques* (Kangaroo Press, 2003).

Eppler, Richard A. and Douglas R., *Glazes and Glass Coatings* (American Ceramic Society, 2000).

Hamer, Frank and Janet, *The Potter's Dictionary of Materials and Techniques* (rev. edn) (Watson-Guptill, 1986).

Hansen, Tony, Ceramic Materials. Info / Ceramic Oxides Database, DigitalFire Corporation, http://ceramic-materials.com

Hopper, Robin, *The Ceramic Spectrum* (2nd edn) (Krause Publications, 2001).

McCann, Michael, *Artist Beware: The hazards in working with all art and craft materials and the precautions every artist and craftsperson should take* (Lyons Press, 2001).

McKee, Charles, *Ceramic Handbook: A guide to glaze calculation, materials and processes* (Star Publishing, 1984).

Parmalee, C.W., *Ceramic Glazes* (2nd edn) (Industrial Publications, 1951).

Piepenburg, Robert, *Raku Pottery* (Pebble Press, 1991).

Rhodes, Daniel, *Clay and Glazes for the Potter* (rev. edn) (Chilton, 1973).

Rossol, Monona, *The Artist's Complete Health and Safety Guide* (Allworth Press, 2002).

Rossol, Monona, *Keeping Clay Work Safe and Legal* (2nd edn) (NCECA, 1996).

Seger, Herman A., *Collected Writings* (vol. 2) (Chemical Publishing, 1902).

Glossary

Acid A chemical compound with a pH of less than 7, or a compound that liberates protons when it interacts with other materials. Acids are chemically the opposite of bases, and the two neutralize each other on contact. Glaze components are described as acidic oxides, neutral oxides and base oxides.

Acute toxicity Denotes a poisonous substance, a compound that will cause serious harm if ingested even once in sufficient quantity.

Alkaline earth metals Glaze oxides related by their chemical structure, behaviour and placement on the periodic table of elements. They include barium, magnesium, calcium and strontium.

Amorphous A compound with a random organisation, lacking specific form. For the ceramicist molten liquid glass represents an amorphous structure, which results from the breakdown of fixed molecular bonds in the various oxides that make it up.

Ball mill A rotary device with glass or porcelain balls for wet-grinding clay and glaze materials into a very fine particle size.

Base unity A phrase referring to the mathematical structure of a glaze formula in which the entire glaze (minus colouring or suspension ingredients) adds up to 100 parts.

Base (caustic base) A chemical compound with a pH greater than 7, or a compound that will liberate electrons and neutralize an acid. Alkaline compounds are chemically basic. Base oxides in glaze chemistry are primarily the fluxing oxides that promote melting of the glass – sodium, potassium, lithium, etc.

Bisque fire The initial ceramic firing, usually to 1000°C (1832°F) or so, to harden a ceramic object and make it easier to handle and glaze (known as bisque ware or bisque).

Blister A glaze flaw resulting in broken bubbles with sharp edges that remain on the surface of the cooled glaze. Blistering is evidence of boiling action in the liquid glaze that is not able to smooth over before the glaze chills.

Burnished A glossy clay surface that is polished by being compressed and rubbed with a smooth stone when nearly or completely dry.

Calcine To fire a raw material, changing the physical properties without altering its chemical make-up. For example, when calcined clay is added to a formula it provides the same alumina and silica, but there is no significant shrinkage on drying.

Carbon-charged A clay body that appears grey or black after absorbing large amounts of free carbon, usually in post-fire reduction.

Casting slip A clay slip formulated with low water content and made fluid through de-flocculation, used primarily for casting forms in plaster moulds.

Ceramic stains Prepared ceramic colourants formulated with one or more raw metallic oxides, often with materials, and fired to fuse and stabilize them. These stains are fritted colourants providing a wide range of predicable hues.

Chronic exposure This refers to long-term, often low-concentration exposure to substances that are not in themselves considered poisonous.

Coefficient of expansion A term referring to the measurable linear expansion (and contraction) of a clay or glaze when heated (and cooled). Differences in the coefficient of expansion between clay and glaze result in glaze-fit problems such as crazing and shivering.

Colouring oxides Metallic oxides such as iron, cobalt, chrome, copper and manganese, used primarily to give colour to a glaze base.

Compression A reference to the physical state of a glaze that is fired on a clay body which has a greater coefficient of expansion (see Shivering).

Cone, Orton firing cone A small pyramidal-shaped cone, manufactured from ceramic materials and designed to melt at a precise degree of heatwork, identified by a sequence of numbers. Orton cones are standard in the USA, whereas Seger cones are widely used in Europe.

Convection The circulatory motion within a liquid glaze that results from temperature and density differentials.

Cratering, Crater glazes A glaze flaw resulting in a lava-like surface composed of many small and large broken bubbles.

Crawling A glaze flaw in which the glaze shrinks into itself during the firing, leaving bare patches of clay visible.

Crazing A glaze flaw in which the glaze shrinks more than the clay body upon cooling. This is also known as a glaze-in-tension, and often results in a network of fine cracks in the glaze.

Crucible A refractory ceramic vessel used for melting glaze materials to produce frits.

Crystallization The formation of crystal structures. A process that may occur upon the cooling of a glaze in which crystalline structures form on the surface of the liquid-glass matrix.

Crystobalite A form of silica with a different molecular arrangement and expansion rate than quartz.

Decomposition (chemical) The breakdown of chemical compounds into their constituent molecules during the firing process.

Devitrification A process during which crystalline development occurs in a cooling glaze causing the glaze to lose its amorphous structure, becoming opaque.

Earthenware A clay or clay body that matures at low temperatures, or finished ware fired to low temperatures, usually below cone 03 (1100°C/2014°F).

Empirical A method for testing and discovery

based on experimentation and observation.

Engobe A ceramic coating normally applied to bisque ware, resulting in a dry surface similar to a vitrified clay slip. Chemically, an engobe is a hybrid mixture of a glaze and slip.

Eutectic A phenomenon in which the melting point of a mixture of two elements is lower than that of either element by itself.

Feldspar A naturally occurring mineral of igneous origin that is used to supply a variety of elements in a glaze formula. Feldspars are fairly complex compounds and usually contain silica, alumina and fluxing oxides, with sodium and potassium being most common.

Firing latitude The range of temperature through which a slip or glaze can be fired with acceptable results.

Flux A flux is an element or compound that promotes melting in a glaze. The action of melting is often referred to as fluxing.

Fluxing oxides Ceramic oxides used primarily to promote melting in a glaze. These include boron, lead, zinc, sodium, potassium, lithium, barium, strontium, calcium and magnesium.

Formula Glaze formulas are also known as glaze recipes.

Frit, glaze frit A mixture of specific raw fluxing oxides and silica and usually alumina, melted together in a crucible and poured as liquid glass into water to chill it. Frits are ground to a fine particle size and used in glazes to introduce particular compounds in insoluble form.

Fritted flux A glaze flux that has been prepared as a frit.

Glaze fit A term used to describe the difference between the coefficient of expansion of a glaze and that of the clay body onto which it is fired. If the difference is too great, problems such as crazing or shivering occur.

Grogged stoneware clay A prepared clay body with a moderately coarse particle size containing ground fire brick (grog), which matures at high temperatures around (1300°C/2380°F).

Inclusion stain A type of manufactured ceramic stain in which fugitive elements such as selenium are stabilized in compounds with zirconium crystals, allowing them to be added to glazes and maintain their colour at a variety of temperatures.

Leaching A process through which a chemical constituent of a glaze may move out of the glaze into its surrounding environment.

Levigation A process of refining or sorting by particle size through the settling of material in water over time.

Lustre finish An iridescent quality to the surface of a glaze, usually resulting from a cooling reduction atmosphere.

Mature The point at which a clay or glaze reaches maximum vitrification before it begins to deform.

Molecular ratio The relative proportion of parts of molecules of various materials in a glaze.

Molochite A white grog made from kaolin.

Monoprinting A type of direct-image transfer in which a unique image is painted onto a glass or plaster surface, then bonded to a paper or clay sheet and lifted off.

Off-gas The liberation of gases from a clay body or glaze. A period toward the end of a glaze firing when the temperature is held steady and the glaze is allowed time to release gases arising from the products of decomposition.

Opacifier Compound(s) added to a glaze to make it appear white and opaque, usually tin oxide or zirconium silicates.

Opalescence A visual characteristic of some glazes, described as milky and semi-opaque, often with a delicate blue tint, and usually resulting from the formation and suspension of many tiny bubbles in the glass matrix.

Overglaze enamels Specialised glazes in a wide range of colours, formulated to melt at very low temperatures, normally applied on top of fired glaze. Enamels are usually stiff and opaque, while china paints are transparent, but both are fired on at very low temperatures (717°C/1323°F).

Oxidize To combine with oxygen. In clay and glazes this refers to the result of normal electric firings and gas firings that allow complete combustion within the kiln.

Porcelain A fine-grained, white and vitrified

clay body based on kaolin and feldspar, fired to approximately cone 10 (1300°C/ 2380°F).

Post-firing reduction A carbon-rich atmosphere created and held around the ware as it cools after the glaze firing, often to create metallic and lustre effects.

Potash (feld)spar A feldspar in which the dominant fluxing oxide is potassium.

Primary clay A raw clay that is mined relatively close to its geologic origins. Primary clays include kaolins and are relatively pure and free of iron contaminants.

Raku firing A rapid, low-temperature firing process that involves removing the ware from the kiln with tongs immediately after it reaches maximum temperature. The ware may then be allowed to cool or treated with post-firing reduction.

Reduced, reduction firing A clay or glaze that has been fired in a reduction firing, usually involving a gas or wood-firing process with insufficient oxygen provided for complete combustion. This results in changes to the colour of certain colouring oxides, notably iron and copper, in the clay and glaze.

Refractory A material that is resistant to heat and melting. This is a relative term, but in studio ceramics if a material shows no signs of melting at stoneware temperatures (1300°C/ 2380°F) it is considered refractory.

Screen-printing A process for transferring an image multiple times, using a fine screen to hold a stencil through which ink, slip or over-glaze enamel may be pressed to form an image.

Secondary clay A raw clay found and mined a considerable distance from its geologic origin. Secondary clays typically have greater contamination with iron and other oxides, like many red earthenwares, and may also have smaller particle sizes like ball clays due to larger particles settling out as they are washed to their final site.

Seger Unity Formula A method of analyzing a glaze formula developed by the German ceramicist Herman Seger, which reduces the constituent parts to their relative ratio of molecules. The unity formula structure stipulates that the total quantity of all the fluxing oxides equals one molecule, and the molecular ratio of alumina and silica are expressed in proportion to that.

Shivering A glaze flaw in which the clay body shrinks more upon cooling than the glaze which covers it. This is also known as a glaze in compression and can result in slivers of the glaze popping off the ware.

Sintered A clay slip or glaze that has undergone the compaction, interaction and initial fusion of particles that occurs in the early portion of the firing process. In a sintered glaze the constituent particles are beginning to fuse at their points of contact but have not begun to melt to any appreciable degree.

Soda firing A medium- to high-temperature firing in which a liquid solution of sodium compounds is sprayed into the kiln, causing the sodium to vaporize and attack the clay, forming a glaze on the ware.

Soda spar A feldspar in which the dominant fluxing oxide is sodium.

Stoneware A clay or clay body that has been or could be fired to a high temperature; also finished ware that has been high fired to cones 5–10 (1200–1300°C/2185–2380°F).

Terra sigillata A very fine clay slip prepared through a settling process in which only the smallest particles are collected and used.

Thermal shock A type of stress on fired ware that occurs due to uneven heating or cooling, most commonly during a critical point in the firing (at about 570°F/1060°F), in which the silica in the clay body ware goes through a sudden expansion (or contraction) known as quartz inversion.

Underglaze A specialized engobe or slip that typically contains a large amount of colouring oxides or ceramic stains, and is applied to the surface of bisque ware prior to glazing.

Viscosity The relative stiffness and resistance to movement of a liquid.

Vitrification The point at which a clay, slip or glaze has reached a glasslike state.

Volatize The process of vaporizing, or becoming a gas.

Suppliers

UK

Bath Potters' Suppplies
Unit 18 Fourth Ave
Westfield Trading Estate
Radstock, Bath BA3 4XE
Tel: 01761 411 077
Fax: 01761 414 115
Email enquiries@bathpotters.demon.co.uk

Briar Wheels & Supplies Ltd
Whitsbury Road
Fordingbridge
Hants SP6 1NQ
Tel: 01425 652991
www. briarwheels.co.uk

Imerys Minerals Ltd
(formerly English China Clays)
John Keay House
St. Austell
Cornwall PL25 4DJ
www.imerys-perfmins.com/eu/home.asp
Tel:01726 818000

Potclays Ltd
Brickkiln Lane
Etruria
Stoke-on-Trent ST4 7BP
Tel: 01782 219816
www.potclays.co.uk

Potterycrafts Ltd
Campbell Road
Stoke-on-Trent ST4 4ET
Tel: 01782 745000
Fax: 01782 746000
www.potterycrafts.co.uk

Scarva Pottery Supplies
Unit 20, Scarva Road Industrial Estate
Banbridge, Co. Down BT32 3QD
Tel: 018206 69699
Fax: 018206 69700
www.scarvapottery.com

U.S.A. and Canada

Alligator Clay Company
2721 W. Perdue Ave,
Baton Rouge,
LA 70184
Tel: 225 932 9457
www.alligatorclay.com

American Art Clay Co.
W.16th Street,
Indianapolis IN 46222
Tel: 317 244 6871
www.amaco.com

Columbus Clay Company
1080 Chambers Road,
Columbus,
OH 43212
Tel: (866) 410 2529
www.columbusclay.com

Laguna Clay Co.
1440 Lomitas Avenue
City of Industry, CA 91746
Tel: 800 452 4862
www.lagunaclay.com

Mile Hi Ceramics Inc.
77 Lipan,
Denver
CO 80223
Tel: (303) 825 4570
www.milehiceramics.com

Minnesota Clay Co.
8001 Grand Avenue South
Bloomington, MN 55420
Tel: 612 884 9101

Tuckers Pottery Supplies Inc.
15 West Pearce St.
Richmond Hill
Ontario, Canada L4B1 H6
Tel: 800 304 6185
www.tuckerspottery.com

Index